KETOGENIC DIET

Better Energy, Performance, and Natural Fuel to Good Health for the Smart

DIANA WATSON

Table of Contents

Index

VIP Subscriber List

Hi Dear Reader, this is Diana! If you like my book and you want to receive the latest tips and tricks on cooking, weight-loss, cookbook recipes and more, do subscribe to my mailing list in the link here! I will then be able to send you the most up-to-date information about my upcoming books and promotions as well! Thank you for supporting my work and happy reading!

Subscriber Form

http://bit.do/dianawatson

Introduction

Congratulations on purchasing the *Ketogenic Diet: Better Energy, Performance, and Natural Fuel to Good Health for the Smart*, and thank you for doing so.

The following chapters will discuss many different ways you can eat healthier using a high-fat diet that remains low in carbohydrates. An extensive amount of research has been provided to prove how this type of plan can improve your health and help you lose the unwanted pounds.

It works using the process of ketosis which will be briefly explained.

There are plenty of books on this subject on the market, thanks again for choosing this one! Every effort was made to ensure it is full of as much useful information as possible; please enjoy!

Chapter 1: The Keto Plan & How it Works

You will soon understand how you can eat most of the foods you always enjoy. You will be able to make some substitutes to get going which are described within this chapter.

Happy Discovery!

Several Types of Keto Diet Plans

- *Plan 1*: You can choose from the standard ketogenic diet (SKD) which consists of high-fat, moderate protein, and is extremely low in carbs.

- *Plan 2*: The cyclical ketogenic diet or CKD is created with 5-keto days trailed by two high-carb days.

- *Plan 3*: The targeted keto diet, which is also called TKD, will provide you with a plan to add carbs to the diet during the times when you are working out.

- *Plan 4*: The high-protein ketogenic diet is very similar to the standard keto plan in all aspects except that it has more protein.

However, let's not get too far ahead of the plan. You need to focus on the first 30 days! The long process to explain each of these types would take another entire book!

Health Benefits from a Ketogenic Diet Plan

These are just a few of the ways you can benefit from remaining on the diet plan. It's hard to believe a diet plan can remedy so many health issues.

Acne: Your insulin levels are lowered by consuming less sugar and eating less processed foods. The acne will begin to clear up as you continue with the plan.

Alzheimer's disease: The symptoms and progression will be slowed.

Lowered Blood Pressure: While using the keto plan; you are experiencing reduced intake of carbs which will reduce your blood pressure levels. It is recommended to seek advice from your regular doctor to see if it is possible to reduce some of your medication while you are on the keto diet. You may also have some dizziness when you first begin the plan which is one of the first indications that the plan is working. The result is a lack of carbohydrates.

Cancer: Slow tumor growths and several other types of cancer have shown improvement with the keto plan.

Diabetes and Pre-diabetes: The main link to pre-diabetes is excess body fat which is removed which is proven by research that insulin sensitivity was improved by as much as 70%.

Epilepsy: Children's research studies have proven the diet works in the reduction of seizure activity.

Gum Disease: The sugar you consume influences the pH balance in your mouth. If you have issues before you begin the plan; you should begin to see a remarkable improvement within approximately three months.

Obesity: When the ketogenic diet plan is followed—the weight will dissolve.

Stiffness and Joint Pain: It is important to continue with the elimination of any grain-based foods. It is believed that the grains are one of the largest factors which cause the pain. Just remember "no grain—no pain."

Thinking is Improved: You might be a bit foggy-minded when you first begin the plan since you will be consuming high-fat foods. After all, your brain is about 60% fat by weight; your thinking skills should improve with the intake of the fatty foods indicated with the keto diet.

The Elements of Ketosis

Ketosis is used to help your burn body fat and drop extra pounds. Proteins will fuel your body to burn the fat—therefore—the ketosis will maintain your muscles and make you less hungry.

Your body will remain healthy and work as it should. If you don't consume enough carbs from your food; your cells will begin to burn fat for the necessary energy instead. Your body will switch over to ketosis for its energy source as your cut back on your calories and carbs.

Two elements that occur when your body doesn't need the glucose:

Lipogenesis: If there is a sufficient supply of glycogen in your liver and muscles, any excess is converted to fat and stored.

Glycogenesis: The excess of glucose converts to glycogen and is stored in the muscles and liver. Research indicates that only about half of your energy used daily can be stored as glycogen.

As a result, your body will have no more food—similar to when you are sleeping—your body burns the fat and creates ketones. These ketones break down the fats, which generate fatty acids, and burn-off in the liver through beta-oxidation.

Simply stated, when you no longer have a supply of glycogen or glucose, ketosis begins and will use the consumed/stored fat as energy.

The Internet provides you with a keto calculator to use at http://keto-calculator.ankerl.com/. You can check your levels when you want to know what essentials your body needs during your diet plan or after. All you need to do is document your personal information such as weight and height. The calculator will provide you with the essential math.

Weight Loss and Protein

Protein needs to be in your plan for these reasons:

Protein is a Fat Burner: Science has proven your body cannot use and burn your fat as energy sources unless you have help from either carbs or protein. The balance of protein must be maintained to preserve your calorie-burning lean muscles.

Protein Saves Your Calories: Protein slows down your digestion process making you feel more satisfied from the foods you eat. During the first cycle of your diet plan; it is imperative that you feel full, so there is no temptation to cheat on the strategy.

Muscle Repair and Growth: Protein should be increased on days when you are more active. It is essential to have a plan on what your meals will consist of with a balance of carbs, proteins, and calories. The balance is what you are attempting to achieve with a focused plan such as the keto diet.

The Role of Calories, Protein, and Carbs

Calories are held within your body with the use of the nutrients of protein, fat, and carbs which your body will use for energy.

Carbohydrates

Your body exchanges one-hundred percent of the carbs into glucose which gives your body an energy boost. About 50% to 60% of your intake of calories is produced by carbs. Carbs stored in your liver as glycogen is released as your body needs it. Glucose is essential for the creation of adenosine triphosphate (ATP) which is an energy molecule. The fuel from glucose is vital for the daily maintenance and activities inside your body. After the liver has reached its maximum capacity for its limits, the excessive carbohydrates turn into fat.

Count Those Carbs

Before you are totally in gear, you need to start carb counting to make sure you keep your body in perfect 'sync' with the plan. Reading the labels may be a bit nerve-racking in the beginning, but after a while, it will be as you have always done it that way.

Remember this Formula: Total Carbs minus (-) Fiber = Net Carbs

A rough estimate will include you consuming between 20 to 30 carbs daily. It is almost a necessity to own a set of food scales to take out the guesswork.

Keep this information in mind before you make the purchase:

- *The Automatic Shut-Off*: Seek a scale that does not have this option. The result could be you being in the midst of a recipe—move the dish—and the scale could reset; NOT.

- *The Tare Function*: When you set a bowl on the scale, the feature will allow you to reset the scale back to zero (0).

- *Removable Plate*: Keep the germs off of the scale by removing the plate. Be sure it will come off to eliminate the bacterial buildup.

- *Seek a Conversion Button*: You need to know how to convert measurements into grams since not all recipes have them listed. The grams keep the system in complete harmony.

Natural Supplements for Ketogenic Dieters

Fermented Foods: Use items, while on the keto plan such as coconut milk kefir, coconut milk, yogurt, pickles, sauerkraut, and kimchi to help with any digestive issues.

Lemon and Lime: Your blood sugar levels will naturally drop with these citric additions, and signal a boost in your liver function. Use them in green juices, with a salad, or with cooked with meats or veggies. The choices are limitless and assist you with the following:

- Reduces toothache pain
- Boosts your immune system
- Relieves respiratory infections
- Balances pH
- Decreases wrinkles and blemishes
- Reduces fever
- Excellent for weight loss
- Flushes out the unwanted, unhealthy materials
- Blood purifier

Apple Cider Vinegar: Who would believe the benefits you can receive from just one to two tablespoons of vinegar in an 8-ounce glass of water would help the process? You can choose the straight up method and skip the water.

These are just a few ways this helps your progress:

- Reduces cholesterol

- Excellent for detoxification

- Helps you to drop the pounds

- Improves your digestion tract

- Helps with sore muscles

- Controls sugar intake/aids in diabetes

- Strengthens your immune system

- A good energy booster

- Balances your inner body system and functions

Cinnamon: Use cinnamon as part of your daily plan to improve your insulin receptor activity. Just put one-half of a teaspoon of cinnamon into a shake or any type of keto dessert. Many of the keto recipes contain the ingredient.

Turmeric: Dating back to Ayurveda and Chinese medicine the is of this Asian orange herb has been known for its anti-inflammatory compounds. Add it to you smoothies, green drinks, meats, or veggies. These are some of its benefits:

- Prevents Alzheimer's disease

- Weight management

- Relieves arthritis

- Reduces your cholesterol levels

- Helps control diabetes

- Improves your digestion

Be Aware of Some Foods and Beverages: Which Ones to Avoid

Agave Nectar: One teaspoon has 5 grams of carbs versus 4 grams in table sugar.

Beans and Legumes: This group to avoid includes peas, lentils, kidney beans, and chickpeas. If you use them, be sure to count the carbs, protein, and fat content.

Cashews and Pistachios: The high carb content should be monitored for these yummy nuts.

Fruits: Raspberries, blueberries, and cranberries contain high sugar contents. In small portions; you can enjoy some strawberries.

Grains and Starches: Avoid wheat-based items such as cereal, rice, or pasta.

Hydrogenated Fats: Cold-pressed items should be
avoided when using vegetable oils such as safflower,
olive, soybean, or flax. Coronary heart disease has been
linked to these fats which also include margarine.

Tomato-based Products: Read the labels because most of
the tomato products contain sugar. If you use them be
sure to account for the sugar content. (The recipes
provided have considered this.)

Chapter 2: The 14-Day Plan

Day One

Breakfast: Keto Scrambled Eggs

Ingredients

3 large eggs

Fresh ground pepper

Coarse salt

1 tablespoon unsalted butter

Instructions

1. Whisk the eggs in a bowl.

2. Use low heat and place the butter into a skillet.

3. Add the eggs. Continue to stir until well-done, usually 1 ½ to 3 minutes.

Serving Portion: Fat: 26.3 g; Carbs 1.8 g; Protein: 17.4 g; Calories: 318

Lunch: Tuna Cheese Melt (Low-Carbs)

Ingredients

2 Pieces of "Oopsie" bread

Ingredients for the Salad

1 to 2 Celery stalks

5 1/3 Tablespoons sour cream or mayonnaise

1 Can tuna (in olive oil)

4 Tablespoons chopped dill pickles

½ teaspoon lemon juice

Pepper and salt to taste

½ minced clove garlic

Toppings

A pinch of paprika powder or cayenne pepper

3 ½ ounces shredded cheese

Serving Ingredients

Olive oil

1/3 Pound leafy greens

"Oopsie" Bread (makes six to 8)

3 Eggs

A pinch of salt

4 ¼ ounces cream cheese

½ teaspoon baking powder

½ Tablespoon ground psyllium husk powder

Instructions

1. Preheat the oven to 350ºF. Put parchment
    paper onto a cookie sheet.

2. Blend all of the salad ingredients.

3. Place the bread slices on the prepared sheet,
    spread the tuna, and sprinkle the cheese on
    top of each slice of bread.

4. Sprinkle some cayenne or paprika powder on
    the sandwich halves and bake in the oven for
    about 15 minutes.

5. Have some leafy greens with a drizzle of olive
    oil.

"Oopsie" Bread Instructions

1. Heat the oven to oven at 300ºF.

2. Begin by separating the egg whites (whites in
    one bowl and yolks in the other).

3. Whisk the egg whites with the salt until peaks
    are formed.

4. Combine the cream cheese and egg yolks—add the baking powder and psyllium seed husk (making it more Oopsie type bread).

5. Blend/fold in the whites into the yolk mixture —keeping out the air in the whites of the eggs.

6. Place six or eight 'oopsies' on the paper-lined sheet.

7. Bake in the center oven rack, usually for 25 minutes or until browned.

Dinner: Chicken Smothered in Creamy Onion Sauce

Ingredients

1 whole green/spring onion

2 tablespoons or 1-ounce butter

4 chicken breast halves (skinless—boneless)

8 ounces sour cream

½ teaspoon sea salt

Note: The chicken should weigh approximately six ounces or 170 g for this recipe.

Instructions

1. In a large pan, melt the butter on the stovetop using the med-high setting. Lower the heat setting to med-low—put the chicken with the butter—cover and cook about ten more minutes.

2. Chop the onion using just the white and green sections.

3. Flip the breasts—cover and simmer—another 8 or 9 minutes (or until completely done).

4. Combine the onion, and continue cooking the chicken for another one or two minutes.

5. Take it off of the burner, and blend in the salt and sour cream.

6. Let the meal rest and flavors blend for five minutes.

Stir well and serve.

Day Two

Breakfast: Mock Mc Griddle Casserole

Ingredients

1 pound breakfast sausage

¼ cup flaxseed meal

1 cup almond flour

10 large eggs

6 tablespoons maple syrup

4 ounces cheese

4 tablespoons butter

¼ teaspoon sage

½ teaspoon each: onion & garlic powder

Instructions

1. Heat the oven to 350ºF. Use parchment paper to line a 9 x 9-inch casserole dish.

2. Using medium heat; start cooking the breakfast sausage on the stove in a skillet.

3. Blend all of the dry (the cheese included) ingredients and add the wet ones.

4. Add four tablespoons of the syrup and blend well.

5. After the sausage is crispy brown—blend all of the ingredients; (the fat too).

6. Pour the mixture into the dish and sprinkle the remainder of the syrup on the top.

7. Bake for 45 to 55 minutes. Remove it and let it cool.

Yields: Eight Servings

Time Saving Tip: The casserole should be easy to remove by using the edge of the parchment paper.

Lunch: Brussels Sprouts with Hamburger Gratin

Ingredients

1 Pound Ground beef

1 Pound Brussels sprouts

½ Pound diced bacon

4 tablespoons sour cream

1/3 Pound shredded cheese

1- ¾ Ounces butter

Pepper and salt to taste

1 tablespoon Italian seasoning

Instructions

1. Cut the Brussels sprouts in half.

2. Preheat the oven to 425ºF/220ºC.

3. Saute the Brussels sprouts and bacon in the butter. Flavor with the sour cream and place in a baking pan/dish.

4. Fry the beef and season with pepper and salt;
   add the herbs and cheese—sprinkling on top of
   the base layer.

5. Bake on the center rack of the oven for fifteen
   minutes.

Serve with a dollop of mayonnaise and a fresh salad.

Yields: Four Servings

Dinner: Squash and Sausage Casserole

Ingredients

1 pound browned sausage

2 large eggs

1 medium zucchini (sliced & cooked)

2 medium summer squash (sliced & cooked)

1 teaspoon salt

½ teaspoon onion powder or ¼ cup dried minced onion

1 cup mayonnaise

1 package sugar substitute (or stevia)

¼ teaspoon pepper

1 ½ cups shredded cheddar cheese (divided)

¼ melted butter

Instructions

1. Pre-set the oven to 350ºF.

2. Blend each of the ingredients except for one-half of a cup of shredded cheese.

3. Put the ingredients into a lightly greased oblong baking plate.

4. Sprinkle the remainder of cheese on the casserole.

5. Bake until lightly browned for approximately thirty minutes.

This casserole will easily serve 12 people with an amazing flavor you won't soon forget!

Day Three

Breakfast: Can't Beat it Porridge

Ingredients

1 cups almond or coconut milk

1 pinch salt

1 Tablespoon each:

- Sunflower seeds

- Chia Seeds

Instructions

1. Using a small saucepan on the stovetop, blend
   each of the components, and bring to a
   boiling. Lower the burner and cook slowly
   until the porridge is the consistency you desire

2. Garnish with some butter or milk. You can also
   add some fresh unsweetened berries or
   cinnamon.

Yields: One Serving

Time Saving Tip: Make it ahead of time using a big glass jar. Fill the jar with the following ingredients and shake them up. Each serving will correspond with three tablespoons for each serving.

These are the ingredients needed for the batch:

1 Tbsp. cinnamon

½ tsp. salt

1 1/4 cup each:

- Sunflower seeds

- Flaxseeds

- Chia seeds

Lunch: Salad From a Jar

Ingredients

1 (4-ounce) rotisserie chicken/smoked salmon/other protein

1 ounce each:

- Cucumber

- Cherry tomatoes

- Leafy greens

- Bell pepper

4 tablespoons olive oil or mayonnaise

½ Scallion

Instructions

1. Chop or shred the veggies and place the leafy greens to the bottom for a crunch followed by the colorful veggies. (You can also use some cauliflower or broccoli for a change of pace.)

2. Top it off with some of the grilled protein of your choice. You can also use cold cuts, tuna fish, mackerel or boiled eggs.

3. Cheese cubes, seeds, nuts, and olives are also healthy and colorful additions.

4. Add a generous amount of mayonnaise or salad dressing and enjoy!

Yields: One Serving

Dinner: Ham and Cheese Stromboli

Ingredients

1 large egg

1 ¼ cups shredded mozzarella cheese

3 tablespoons coconut flour

4 tablespoons almond flour

4 ounces of ham

1 teaspoon Italian seasoning

3 ½ ounces cheddar cheese

Instructions

1. Preheat the oven to 400ºF.

2. Melt the mozzarella cheese in the microwave for one minute/alternating at ten-second intervals; stirring until melted.

3. In a mixing bowl, blend the coconut and almond flour with the seasonings.

4. Toss in the mozzarella on the top and work it in.

5. After the cheese has cooled; beat the egg and combine everything

6. On a flat surface; put some parchment paper, and add the mixture.

7. Use a rolling pin or your hands to flatten the mix.

8. Place several diagonal lines using a knife or pizza cutter. (Leave a row of approximately four inches wide in the center.

9. Alternate the layers using the cheddar and ham on the uncut space of dough until you have used all of the filling.

10. Bake for 15 to 20minutes or it is browned.

Day Four

Breakfast: Frittata with Cheese and Tomatoes

Ingredients

6 eggs

2/3 cup soft cheese (ex. Feta 3 ½ ounces or 100 g)

½ medium white onion (1.9 ounces or 55 g)

2/3 cup halved cherry tomatoes

2 tablespoons chopped herbs (ex. basil or chives)

1 tablespoon ghee/butter

Instructions

1. Heat the oven broiler to 400ºF.

2. Place the onions on a greased, hot iron skillet, and
   cook with ghee/butter until slightly brown.

3. In a separate container, crack the eggs and add
   the salt, pepper, or add herbs of your choice.
   Whisk and add to the onion pan.

4. Cook until the edges begin to get brown. Top with
   the cheese and tomatoes.

5. Put the pan in the broiler for five to seven minutes
   or until done.

Lunch: Chicken—Broccoli—Zucchini Boats

For a variety textures as well as flavors to spice up lunch;
this is the one!

Ingredients

6 ounces shredded chicken

2 tablespoons butter

2 hollowed-out zucchini (10 ounces)

3 ounces shredded cheddar cheese

1 stalk of green onion

1 cup broccoli

2 tablespoons sour cream

Instructions

1. Heat the oven temperature to 400ºF.

2. Slice the zucchini lengthwise and scoop most of the insides out until you have a shell of approximately ½ to 1 cm. thick.

3. Melt one tablespoon of the butter into each boat, flavor with a dash of pepper and salt, and bake them for around twenty minutes.

4. Shred the chicken, cut the broccoli florets into small pieces, and measure out six ounces of cheese. Blend in with the sour cream.

5. Remove the zucchini shells when done and add the mixture.

6. Sprinkle each of them with the remainder of the cheese.

7. Bake for another ten or fifteen minutes until the cheese is browned and melted.

8. Use a bit of sour cream, mayonnaise, or chopped onion as a garnish.

Dinner: Steak-Lovers Slow-Cooked Chili

Ingredients for Chili:

1 cup beef or chicken stock

½ cup sliced leeks

2 ½ pounds (1-inch cubes) steak

2 cups whole tomatoes (canned with juices)

1 tablespoon chili powder

½ tsp. salt

1/8 tsp. ground black pepper

¼ tsp. ground cayenne pepper

½ tsp. cumin

Optional Toppings

1 teaspoon fresh chopped cilantro

2 tablespoons sour cream

¼ cup shredded cheddar cheese

½ avocado (cubed or sliced)

Instructions

1. Place all of the items except the topping fixings into the slow cooker.

2. Set the cooker on the high setting for about six hours.

Yields: Twelve Servings

Serving Portion: 1: Fat: 26.0 g; Carbs 3.3 g; Protein: 38.4 g; Calories: 321

Servings with Toppings: Serving Portion: 1: Fat: 41.32 g; Carbs 13.49 g; Protein: 32.47 g; Calories: 540.33

Day 5

Breakfast: Brownie Muffins

Ingredients

½ tsp. salt

1 cup flaxseed meal

¼ cup cocoa powder

½ Tbsp. baking powder

1 Tbsp. cinnamon

2 Tbsp. coconut oil

1 large egg

1 tsp. vanilla extract

¼ cup sugar-free caramel syrup

½ cup pumpkin puree

¼ cup slivered almonds

1 tsp. apple cider vinegar

Instructions

1. Heat the oven temperature at 350ºF.

2. In a deep mixing bowl—combine all of the ingredients—mixing well.

3. Use six paper liners in the muffin tin, and add ¼ cup of the batter to each one.

4. Sprinkle several almonds on the tops, pressing gently.

5. Bake approximately fifteen minutes. It is done when the top is set.

Serving Portion: 1 muffin (The recipe serves six): Fat: 13.4 g; Carbs 8.2 g; Protein: 7 g; Calories: 183.3

Lunch: Bacon-Avocado-Goat Cheese Salad

Ingredients

½ Pound bacon

½ Pound goat cheese

4 ounces walnuts

2 avocados

4 ounces arugula lettuce

Ingredients for the Dressing

7 ½ tablespoons mayonnaise

Juice of ½ of a lemon

2 tablespoons heavy whipping cream

7 ½ tablespoons olive oil

Instructions

1. Preheat the oven temperature to 400ºF/200ºC.

2. Prepare a baking dish with some parchment paper.

3. Slice the goat cheese into ½-inch round slices and put in the baking dish. Place on the upper rack of the oven.

4. Pan-fry the bacon until crunchy.

5. Cut the avocados and place on top of a bed of lettuce, add the bacon, cheese, and nuts to the top of your creation.

6. Make the dressing using a stick blender. Sprinkle in a dash of pepper, salt, or a few fresh herbs.

Yields: Four Servings

Dinner: Tenderloin Stuffed Keto Style

Ingredients

2 pounds pork tenderloin or venison

½ cup feta cheese

½ cup gorgonzola cheese

1 teaspoon chopped onion

2 tablespoons crushed almonds

2 garlic cloves, minced

½ teaspoon each: fresh ground black pepper and sea salt

Instructions

1. Preheat the grill.

2. Form a pocket in the tenderloin.

3. Mix the cheeses, almonds, garlic, and onions.

4. Stuff the pocket, and seal using a skewer.

5. Grill until its desired doneness.

Yields: Eight Servings

Serving Portion: 1: Fat: 6.2 g; Carbs 2.9 g; Protein: 28.8 g; Calories: 194

Day 6

Breakfast: Sausage—Feta—Spinach Omelet

Ingredients

½ tablespoon extra-virgin olive oil

2 sausage links

3 large eggs

¼ cup Half & Half

1 cup spinach

1 tablespoon feta cheese

Note: You will need two skillets for this yummy omelet!

Instructions

1. Use medium heat for both pans, and pour olive oil in one of the two.

2. In a small dish, use the Half & Half and mix with the eggs—add the seasonings—and scramble.

3. In the clean pan, cook the sausage.

4. Sauté the spinach in the oiled pan—add a pinch of salt and pepper if desired.

5. After both have finished cooking; put them together in a bowl.

6. Transfer the olive oiled pan to the sausage fat pan —and add the eggs.

7. When the edges begin to cook—add the spinach, sausage, and cheese. Cook another minute—flip the omelet. Cook another two to three minutes.

8. Cover one pan with the other and let the combo steam.

9. Remove and enjoy your masterpiece!

Serving Portion: Fat: 43 g; Carbs 3 g; Protein: 31 g; Calories: 535

Lunch: Pancakes with Cream-Cheese Topping

Don't be alarmed, this is an excellent choice for any time and is so healthy.

Ingredients

8 ¾ ounces cottage cheese

5 eggs

1 tablespoon ground psyllium husk powder

A pinch of salt

For Frying: Coconut oil or butter

Ingredients for the Topping

2 tablespoons red or green pesto

½ pound (8 ounces) ricotta or cream cheese

2 tablespoons olive oil

Ground black pepper and Sea Salt

½ thinly sliced red onion

Instructions

1. Combine one tablespoon of the olive oil with the pesto and cream cheese; set aside.

2. Using a hand blender, mix the salt, cottage cheese, eggs, and husk powder; blend until smooth. Let rest for ten minutes.

3. On the stovetop using the medium heat setting; heat two tablespoons of the oil or butter.

4. Drop several dollops of the cheese batter (2 to 3 inches in diameter), frying the pancakes a few minutes per side.

5. Serve with a few red onion slices with a drizzle of oil, pepper, and salt. You can also use fresh herbs, smoked fish roe or chopped chives.

Dinner: Skillet Style Sausage and Cabbage Melt

Ingredients

4 spicy Italian chicken sausages

2 tablespoons coconut oil

½ cup diced onion

1 ½ cups purple cabbage

1 ½ cups green cabbage

2 tablespoons chopped fresh cilantro

2-1-ounce slices Colby jack cheese

Instructions

1. Start by removing the sausage casings and rough-chopping them. Shred the cabbage and chop the onions.

2. Add the coconut oil, cabbage, and onion in a large skillet using the med-high setting for approximately eight minutes (the veggies should be tender).

3. Blend the cheese and cover.

4. Turn the heat off and let it rest five minutes as the cheese melts.

5. When it is time to serve—stir gently and add the cilantro.

Yields: Four Servings

Serving Portion: 1: Fat: 14.62 g; Carbs 3.52 g; Protein: 18.26 g; Calories: 231

Day 7

Breakfast: Tapas

Have a great mixture!

Ingredients

Cold Cuts:

- Prosciutto

- Serrano ham

- Salami

- Chorizo

Cheeses:

- Gouda

- Parmesan

- Mozzarella

- Cheddar

Veggies:

- Pickled cucumbers

- Peppers

- Radishes

- Cucumbers

Avocado with pepper and homemade mayonnaise

Fresh Basil

Splash of fresh squeezed lemon juice

Nuts:

- Hazelnuts

- Almonds

- Walnuts

Instructions

1. Cut all of the ingredients into cubes or sticks
   and split the avocado cutting its fruit into
   small wedges.

2. Blend with four ounces of mayonnaise pepper
   and maybe a splash of lemon juice

3. Use the avocado shells for the serving platter.

Yields: Four Servings

Lunch: Tofu—Bok-Choy Salad

Tofu Ingredients:

15 ounces extra firm tofu

2 teaspoons minced garlic

Juice from ½ a lemon

1 tablespoon each:

- sesame oil

- water

- soy sauce

- rice wine vinegar

Bok Choy Salad Ingredients:

2 tablespoons soy sauce

1 stalk green onion

2 tablespoons chopped cilantro

9 ounces bok choy

3 tablespoons coconut oil

1 tablespoon Sambal Olek

Juice of ½ of a lime

1 tablespoon peanut butter

7 drops liquid Stevia

Instructions

1. Press the tofu in towels for approximately five to six hours to dry.

2. Combine each of the marinade ingredients.

3. When dry; chop the tofu into squares and put in a plastic container/bag with the marinade sauce.

4. Leave it to sit for at least thirty minutes—preferably overnight.

5. Heat the oven to 350ºF. Bake for 30 to 35 minutes on a parchment paper-lined baking dish or a Silpat (non-stick baking sheet with a blend of fiberglass mesh and silicone).

6. In the interim, combine the dressing ingredients (except for the bok choy) in a mixing dish. Toss in the onion and cilantro.

7. Chop the bok choy as you would cabbage, into small slices.

8. Remove the tofu—combine, and enjoy.

Note: Bok choy is a Chinese vegetable.

Serving Portion: Fat: 35 g; Carbs 7.3 g; Protein: 25.0 g; Calories: 442.3

Dinner: Hamburger Stroganoff

Ingredients

8 ounces sliced mushrooms

1 pound ground beef

2 minced cloves of garlic

2 Tbsp. butter

1 ¼ cups sour cream

1/3 cup water or dry white wine

1 tsp. lemon juice

¼ tsp. paprika

1 tsp. dried parsley

Substitute: You may also use one tablespoon fresh chopped parsley.

Instructions

1. Sauté the onions and garlic in a skillet prepared using one tablespoon of butter.

2. Mix in the beef into the pan— sprinkle with pepper and salt if desired. Cook until done and set to the side.

3. Use the remainder of the butter, the mushrooms, and the wine/water, and add them to the pan. Cook until half of the liquid is reduced and the mushrooms are soft.

4. Take them off the burner—add the paprika and sour cream.

5. On low heat stir in the meat and lemon juice.

Use additional spices for flavoring if desired.

Serving Portion: 1 (272 g): Fat: 28.1 g; Carbs 6.1 g; Protein: 38.7 g; Calories: 447

Day 8

Breakfast: Cheddar—Jalapeno Waffles

Ingredients

3 large eggs

1 small jalapeno

3 ounces cream cheese

1 tablespoon coconut flour

1-ounce cheddar cheese

1 teaspoon each:

- baking powder
- Psyllium husk powder

Instructions

1. Combine all of the ingredients using an immersion blender (except for the jalapeno and cheese) until it has a smooth texture.

2. Add the cheese and jalapeno; blend and pour into the waffle iron.

3. You can garnish with your favorite ingredients in about five or six minutes total

Note: Psyllium husk is a native of Pakistan, Bangladesh, and India. It is available online at several locations

Serving Portion: 2 waffles: Fat: 28 g; Carbs 6 g; Protein: 16 g; Calories: 338

Lunch: Salmon Tandoori with Cucumber Sauce

Ingredients

1 ½ Pounds Salmon (In pieces)

2 tablespoons coconut oil

1 tablespoon tandoori seasoning

Ingredients for the Cucumber Sauce

½ cup shredded cucumber

1 ¼ cup sour cream or mayonnaise

2 minced garlic cloves

Juice of ½ of a lime

Optional: ½ teaspoon salt

Ingredients for the Crispy Salad

3 ½ ounces arugula lettuce

3 scallions

1 yellow pepper

Juice of 1 lime

2 avocados

Instructions

1. Preheat the oven to 350ºF.

2. Mix the tandoori seasoning and the 2 tablespoons of oil to coat the salmon.

3. Bake the salmon for fifteen to twenty minutes.

4. Combine the lime juice, garlic, cucumber (blot the water out with paper towels first), and sour cream/mayonnaise in a mixing dish.

5. Prepare the salad ingredients and enjoy.

Yields: Four Servings

Dinner: Ground Beef Stir Fry

Ingredients

300 g (approximately 10 ½ ounces) ground beef

5 medium brown mushrooms

½ cup broccoli

2 leaves kale

½ medium Spanish onion

1 Tbsp. coconut oil

½ medium red pepper

1 Tbsp. cayenne pepper

1 Tbsp. Chinese Five Spices

Note: McCormick was used for the Five Spices

Instructions

1. Prepare the vegetables—slice the mushrooms—
    chop the broccoli.

2. Heat a frying pan on the stovetop using the med-
    high setting. Pour in the oil and toss in the onions.
    Cook for an additional minute.

3. Blend the remainder of the vegetables and cook an additional two minutes—stirring often.

4. Combine the spices and beef—lower the heat to medium—and continue cooking for approximately two more minutes.

5. Cover the pan and cook for five or ten more minutes until the beef is done.

Serving Portion: 1 (Recipe is for three servings): Fat: 18 g; Carbs 7 g; Protein: 29 g; Calories: 307

Day 9

Breakfast: Cheddar and Sage Waffles

Ingredients

1 1/3 coconut flour

1 teaspoon ground sage

½ teaspoon salt

¼ teaspoon garlic powder

3 teaspoons baking powder

2 cups canned coconut milk

½ cup water

3 tablespoons melted coconut oil

1 cup shredded cheddar cheese

2 eggs

Instructions

1. Prepare the waffle iron on the required manufacturer's setting. Grease the iron (top and bottom).

2. Blend all of the seasonings, flour, and baking powder in a container.

3. Mix the wet ingredients, stirring until the batter becomes stiff. Blend in the cheese.

4. Scoop out a one-third cup of the batter and place in each section of the iron.

5. Depending on how you like your waffles; you can run them through two cycles on the iron if you want it crispier.

Serving Portion: 1 waffles (The recipe serves 12): Fat: 17.21 g; Carbs 9.2 g; Protein: 6.52 g; Calories: 213.97

Lunch: Crispy Shrimp Salad on an Egg Wrap

Ingredients for the Wraps

1-ounce butter

4 eggs

Pepper and salt to taste

Shrimp Salad Ingredients

6 ounces shrimp

2 avocados

1/2 of an apple/handful of radishes

1 teaspoon lime juice

1 celery stalk

1 cup mayonnaise

1 red chili pepper

8 tablespoons fresh parsley or cilantro

Instructions for the Wrap

1. Cook and peel the shrimp. Finely chop the red chili pepper and fresh cilantro/parsley.

2. Whip the eggs with the pepper and salt.

3. Using a medium frying pan, melt the butter. Empty half of the egg batter until the egg gets firm, and repeat for the second one.

Instructions for the Salad

1. Slice the avocado and scoop out providing you with ½-inch cubes. Place them in a dish and

give a fresh squeeze of juice over them and mix.

2. Dice the apple and thinly slice the celery, putting them with the avocado. Blend in the peppers, cilantro/parsley, and mayonnaise.

3. Combine well and gently stir in the shrimps. Add more salt if desired.

Yields: Two Servings

This is one of those meals that can be enjoyed with leafy greens or alone. Add a couple of boiled eggs in place of the wrap for another healthy choice.

Dinner: Bacon Wrapped Meatloaf

Ingredients

1 finely chopped yellow onion

1 ½ Pounds ground lamb, poultry, pork *or* beef

2 tablespoons butter

8 tablespoons heavy whipping cream

1 egg

6 ¾ tablespoons shredded cheese

1 tablespoon dried basil/oregano

1 tsp. salt

½ tsp. black pepper

7 ¾ ounces sliced bacon

Optional: ½ tablespoon tamari soy sauce

For the Gravy: 1 ¼ cups heavy whipping cream

Instructions

1. Preheat the oven to 400ºF/200ºC.

2. Saute the onion in a pan with the butter, but don't brown it.

3. Combine the meat in a container, adding all of the remainders of ingredients but omit the bacon. Don't over-work it, but blend the ingredients well, making a loaf.

4. Bake it in the center of the oven for approximately 45 minutes. You can use some aluminum foil to cover the meatloaf, just in case, the bacon begins to scorch.

5. Reserve any of the accumulated juices and make the gravy, blending it with the cream in a small saucepan.

6. Let the mixture come to a boil using low heat until it is creamy and the right texture, usually for approximately ten to fifteen minutes.

7. Spice it up with a drizzle of tamari soy sauce for a bit of flavor.

8. Have some cauliflower or broccoli on the side with some butter. It is all up to you to decide on the veggie choices.

Yields: Four Servings

Day 10

Breakfast: Omelet Wrap with Avocado & Salmon

Ingredients

3 large eggs

½ package smoked salmon (100 g or 1.8 ounces)

½ avocado (3.5 ounces or 100 g)

1 spring onion (1/2 ounce or 15 g)

2 tablespoons cream cheese (full-fat—2.3 ounces or 64 g)

2 tablespoons chives (freshly chopped)

1 tablespoon butter or ghee

Instructions

1. In a mixing bowl—add a pinch of pepper and salt along with the eggs. Use a fork or whisk—mixing them well. Blend the chives and cream cheese.

2. Prepare the salmon and avocado (peel and slice).

3. In a sauté pan, melt the butter/ghee, and add the egg mixture. Cook until fluffy.

4. Put the omelet on a serving dish, and spoon the mixture of cheese over it.

5. Sprinkle the onion, prepared avocado, and salmon into the wrap.

Close and enjoy!

Serving Portion: Fat: 66.9g; Carbs 13.3 g; Protein: 36.9 g

Lunch: Tuna Avocado Melt

Ingredients

1-10 - ounce can drained tuna

1 medium cubed avocado

¼ cup mayonnaise

1/3 cup almond flour

¼ teaspoon onion powder

¼ cup parmesan cheese

½ teaspoon garlic powder

1/2 cup coconut oil (for frying)

Instructions

1. In a mixing container, blend all of the ingredients except for the coconut oil and avocado. Fold the cubed avocado into the tuna.

2. Make balls and coat each one with the almond flour.

3. Use the medium heat setting and put the oil in a pan—mix the tuna—and continue cooking until brown.

Note: Some people like to use this as a casserole dish.

Yields: Twelve Servings

Per Serving Portion: Fat: 11.8 g; Carbs 2.0 g; Protein: 6.2 g; Calories: 134.7

Dinner: Hamburger Patties with Fried Cabbage

Ingredients for the Hamburger Patties

1 egg

1 ½ Pounds ground beef

3 ¼ ounces feta cheese

1 tsp. salt

¼ tsp. ground black pepper

1 ¾ ounces finely- chopped, fresh parsley

1-ounce butter

1 tablespoon olive oil

Ingredients for the Gravy

1 ¾ - Ounces fresh (coarsely chopped) parsley

1 ¼ cups heavy whipping cream

Pepper and Salt

2 tablespoons tomato paste

Ingredients for the Green Cabbage

4 ¼ ounces butter

1 ½ Pounds shredded green cabbage

Pepper and Salt

Instructions

1. Form eight oblong patties by blending all of the ingredients listed under the hamburger patties.

2. Using the med-high setting on the stovetop, prepare a skillet with olive oil and butter and fry the patties for a minimum of ten minutes.

3. Empty the whipping cream and tomato paste
   into the mixture—stir—and let them blend.

Serve with some parsley for garnishment.

Instructions for Butter-fried Green Cabbage

1. Use a food processor or knife to shred the
   cabbage.

2. Prepare a frying pan with the butter and sauté
   the cabbage for approximately fifteen minutes
   on the med-high setting.

3. Reduce the heat for the last five minutes (or
   so)—stirring regularly.

Variations: You can also enjoy this with whatever you
desire, including spinach, carrots, mushrooms, acorn
squash, or corn.

Yields: Four Servings

Day 11

Breakfast: The Breadless Breakfast Sandwich

Ingredients

4 Eggs

1-ounce ham/pastrami cold cuts

2 tablespoons butter

2 ounces of edam/provolone/cheddar cheese

Several drops of Worcestershire or Tabasco sauce

Pepper and salt to taste

Instructions

1. Cut the cheese into thick slices.

2. Prepare a frying pan over medium heat. Fry the eggs over-easy with a pinch of pepper and salt.

3. Add the choice of meat onto the two eggs, a layer of cheese, and the egg for the top of the 'bun.'

4. Give the sandwich a splash of Worcestershire sauce/Tabasco and serve. You can also use some French Dijon mustard to complement the ham.

Yields: Two Servings

Lunch: Thai Fish With Coconut & Curry

Ingredients

1 ½ Pounds whitefish/salmon

4 tablespoons butter/ghee

Pepper and salt

1 to 2 tablespoons green/red curry paste

8 tablespoons fresh chopped cilantro

1 can coconut cream

1 Pound broccoli/cauliflower

For Greasing the Dish: Olive oil/butter

Instructions

1. Grease a baking dish. Preheat the oven to 400ºF.

2. Place the salmon/fish in a dish where there is not any extra space between the dish and fish (not meant as a rhyme).

3. Place a dab of butter on each piece along with a shake of pepper and salt.

4. Combine the chopped cilantro, curry paste and coconut cream in a small container. Pour it over the fish.

5. Bake until the fish is falling apart done, usually about twenty minutes.

6. Boil the broccoli/cauliflower in water (lightly salted) for several minutes as a side dish.

Yields: Four Servings

Dinner: Keto Tacos or Nachos

Ingredients

500 g or 17.6 ounces ground beef

1 medium white onion (3.0 ounces)

4 tacos

1 teaspoon chili powder

2 garlic cloves

½ teaspoon ground cumin

2 teaspoons extra-virgin coconut oil or ghee

1 tablespoon unsweetened tomato puree

1 cup water (8 ounces)

½ teaspoon salt—more or less

Cayenne pepper or freshly ground black pepper

Topping Ingredients

1 small head of lettuce (approximately 3.5 ounces or 100 g)

1 cup or 5.3 ounces cherry tomatoes

1 medium avocado (7.1 ounces or 200 g)

Optional Toppings

4 tablespoons sour cream

1 cup grated cheese

Veggies including cabbage, cucumbers, or peppers

Instructions

1. Using med-high, add some butter/ghee in a frying pan; toss in the onion. Sauté until brown and mix in the beef, continue cooking until the beef is done.

2. Add the cumin and chili powder. (You can substitute with 1 ½ teaspoon of paprika.)

3. Pour in the water and add the tomato puree. Also add pepper, and salt if you like for additional flavoring.

4. Continue cooking until the meat is done and approximately ¼ of the sauce is reduced. Set to the side and prepare the vegetable topping.

5. Use the meat mixture to stuff the shells. Garnish with some of the tomatoes, lettuce, and avocado.

6. As an option, you can add a bit of sour cream or cheddar cheese.

Note: You may use this as a tasty taco or on the side with the meat as the centerfold for the remainder of the veggies.

The choice is all yours!

Day 12

Breakfast: Scrambled Eggs With Halloumi Cheese

Ingredients

5 to 6 eggs

3 ½ ounces diced Halloumi cheese

4 ½ ounces diced bacon

8 tablespoons each:

- Pitted olives

- Chopped fresh parsley

Pepper and Salt to taste

2 scallions

2 tablespoons olive oil

Instructions

1. Dice the bacon and cheese.

2. Over the stovetop, use the medium-high setting; pour the oil into a frying pan. Add the

scallions, cheese, and bacon—sauté until
browned.

3. Whip/Whisk the eggs, pepper, salt, and parsley
    in a mixing container.

4. Pour the mixture into the pan over the cheese
    and bacon.

5. Reduce the heat—toss in the olives and sauté
    for several minutes.

6. All Ready! You can enjoy this with or without a
    salad.

Yields: Two Servings

Lunch: Salmon with Spinach and Chili Tones

Ingredients

1 tablespoon chili paste

1 ½ Pounds Salmon (in pieces)

1 cup sour cream/mayonnaise

1 ¾ cup olive oil/butter

1 Pound fresh spinach

4 tablespoons grated parmesan cheese

Pepper and Salt

Instructions

1. Place the oven setting to 400ºF/200ºC. Use some cooking oil to coat a baking dish/pan.

2. Flavor the salmon with the pepper and salt. Place in the dish skin side down.

3. Blend the chili paste, sour cream/mayonnaise, and parmesan cheese and spread it on the filets.

4. Bake until the salmon is done—usually fifteen to twenty minutes.

5. In the meantime, sauté the spinach until it wilts using the oil/butter.

Yields: Four Servings

Dinner: Chicken Stuffed Avocado—Cajun Style

Ingredients

1 ½ cups cooked chicken (7.4 ounces or 210 g)

2 medium or 1 large avocados (10.6 ounces or 300 g)

2 tablespoons cream cheese/sour cream

2 tablespoons lemon juice (fresh)

¼ cup mayonnaise

½ teaspoon each: onion powder & garlic powder

¼ teaspoon each: salt and cayenne pepper

1 teaspoon each: paprika and dried thyme

Instructions

1. Shred the chicken into small pieces.

2. Blend all of the ingredients—saving the salt and lemon juice until last.

3. Leave one-half to one-inch of the avocado flesh—scoop the middle. Remove the seeds.

4. Cut the center/scooped pieces of avocado into small pieces and fill each of the halves with the mixture of chicken.

Yields: Two Servings

Serving Portion: Fat: 50.6 g; Carbs 16.4 g; Protein: 34.5 g

Day 13

Breakfast: Western Omelet

Ingredients

2 tablespoons sour cream/heavy whipping cream

6 eggs

Pepper and Salt

2 ounces butter

3 ½ ounces shredded cheese

5 ounces of ham

½ each:

- Finely chopped green bell peppers

- Finely chopped yellow onion

Instructions

1. Whisk the sour cream/cream and eggs until fluffy. Flavor with the pepper and salt. Add half of the cheese and combine.

2. Melt the butter on the stovetop on the medium heat setting. Sauté the peppers, onions, and ham for just a few minutes.

3. Pour the batter in and fry until the omelet is almost firm.

4. Lower the heat and Sprinkle the remainder of the cheese on top of your masterpiece. Fold the omelet right away.

Have a fresh green salad as a perfect brunch touch!

Yields: Two Servings

Lunch: Tortilla Ground Beef Salsa

Ingredients

1 ½ Pounds ground lamb/beef

8 to 12 low-carb tortilla breads

2 tablespoons olive oil

1 cup of water

Tex-Mex seasoning (see below)

 1 teaspoon salt

Shredded leafy greens

17 to 27 tablespoons shredded cheese

Salsa Ingredients

1 to 2 diced tomatoes

2 avocados

1 tablespoon olive oil

Juice of 1 lime

8 tablespoons fresh cilantro

Pepper and Salt

Tex-Mex Seasoning

2 tsp. each:

- Paprika powder

- Chili powder

1 to 2 tsp. garlic/onion powder

1 tsp. ground cumin

A pinch of cayenne pepper

Optional: 1 tsp. salt

Instructions

1. Prepare two batches of low-carb tortilla bread (see below).

2. Chop the cilantro. Take out the beef so it can become room temperature. Cold meats can have an effect on the cooking times, and it is more of a boil, not a fry.

3. On the stovetop, heat the oil using a large pan. Toss in the beef, and cook for around ten minutes.

4. Add the salt, water, and taco seasoning to the beef and simmer until most of the liquid has evaporated.

5. Meanwhile, prepare the salsa with all of the ingredients.

6. Serve on the tortilla bread with some shredded cheese along with the leafy greens.

Yields: Four Servings

Low-Carb Tortillas

Ingredients

2 egg whites

2 eggs

6 ounces cream cheese

1 tablespoon coconut flour

1 to 2 teaspoons ground psyllium husk powder

½ teaspoon salt

Instructions

1. Heat the oven to 400ºF. Prepare two baking sheets with parchment paper.

2. Whip the eggs and whites until fluffy. Blend in the cream cheese and whisk until creamy.

3. Combine the coconut flour, psyllium powder, and salt in a small container. Add the flour mixture for the batter a spoon at a time.

4. Spread out the batter on the baking tins, spreading thin, about ¼-inch thick. You can make two rectangles or four to six circles.

5. Bake until the tortilla begins to brown around the edges, usually about five minutes (or so).

6. Serve with some of your *Tex-Mex Ground Beef and Salsa*.

Yields: Two Servings

Dinner: Fish Casserole with Mushrooms

Ingredients

1 Pound mushrooms

3 ¼ ounces butter

2 Tbsp. fresh parsley

1 t. salt

Pepper (to taste)

2 C. heavy whipping cream

2 tablespoons fresh parsley

2 to 3 Tbsp. Dijon mustard

1 ½ Pounds white fish (Ex. Cod)

½ Pound shredded cheese

1 1/3 pounds cauliflower/broccoli

3 ¼ ounces olive oil/butter

Instructions

1. Heat the oven to 350ºF. Lightly grease a baking dish for the fish.

2. Slice the mushrooms into wedges. *Sauté* in a pan with the butter, pepper, salt, and other herbs.

3. Empty the mustard and cream into the mixture and reduce the heat. Simmer for five to ten minutes until the sauce thickens.

4. Flavor the fish with the pepper and salt and add it to the prepared container. Sprinkle with ¾ of the cheese. Pour the creamed mushroom mixture over it and the rest of the cheese as a topping.

5. Bake approximately thirty minutes if the fish are frozen (less if not). After 20 minutes, test the fish to see if it flakes apart easily.

Remember, the fish will cook for several minutes after it is removed from the oven.

6. Prepare the cauliflower into small florets, removing the leaves and stalks. You can use the entire broccoli by cutting it into rods/lengthwise.

7. Boil the veggie of choice, drain and add some butter/olive oil.

8. Coarsely mash with a fork or wooden spoon; adding some pepper and salt, and serve with your fish.

Yields: Four Servings

Day 14

Breakfast: Blueberry Smoothie

Smoothie Ingredients

1 C. fresh or frozen blueberries

1 2/3 C. coconut milk

1 Tbsp. lemon juice

½ tsp. vanilla extract

Instructions

1. Put all of the ingredients into a tall beaker. Mix using a hand mixer.

2. Pour the lemon juice in for additional flavoring.

Notes: You can substitute 1 ¼ cups of Greek yogurt for a dairy option and adjust with a small amount of water if you are searching for more liquid consistency. Add 1 tablespoon of a healthy oil such as coconut for more satiety.

Yields: Two Servings

Lunch: Cheeseburger

Ingredients

7 ounces shredded cheese

1 ½ Pounds ground beef

2 teaspoons each:

- Onion powder

- Garlic powder

- Paprika

For Frying

2 tablespoons fresh oregano

Finely chopped butter

Salsa

2 scallions

2 tomatoes

1 avocado

Fresh Cilantro (to taste)

Salt

1 tablespoon olive oil

Toppings

- Lettuce

- Cooked bacon

- Dijon mustard

- Mayonnaise

- Pickled jalapenos

- Dill pickle

Instructions

1. Chop all of the salsa ingredients in a small container and set to the side.

2. Combine all of the seasonings and ½ of the cheese into the beef mixture.

3. Prepare four burgers and grill or pan fry to your liking—adding cheese at the end of the cooking cycle.

4. Serve on the bed of lettuce with some mustard and a dill pickle.

Yields: Four Servings

Dinner: Turkey with Cream Cheese Sauce

Ingredients

1 1/3 Pounds turkey breast

2 tablespoons butter

2 cups heavy whipping cream/sour cream

7 ounces cream cheese

Pepper and salt

1 tablespoon tamari soy sauce

6 ¾ tablespoons small capers

Instructions

1. Heat the oven to 350ºF.

2. *Sprinkle the turkey with pepper and salt for seasoning.*

3. *Add the butter to a frying pan. Sauté the turkey until golden. Place in the oven to finish cooking.*

4. *Using a small pan, combine the heavy cream/sour cream and cream cheese, bringing it to a boil; lower the heat and cook slowly for a few minutes.*

5. *On high heat in a small pan, use a small amount of butter or oil to fry the capers or enjoy them fresh.*

6. *When the turkey breast and veggies are done, add the sauce and capers on top of the turkey and serve along with some side dishes such as cauliflower or broccoli.*

Yields: Four Servings

Chapter 3: Additional Breakfast Recipes

Chia Pudding

Ingredients

1 cup light coconut milk

¼ cup chia seeds

½ tablespoon light corn syrup

Instructions

1. Combine all of the ingredients in a small mason jar or bowl.

2. Refrigerate overnight. It is ready when the seeds have gelled, and the pudding is thick.

3. Add some nuts and fresh fruit and 'dive in.'

Cow-time Breakfast Skillet

Ingredients

2 medium diced sweet potatoes

1 Pound breakfast sausage

5 eggs

Handful of cilantro

1 diced avocado

Hot sauce

Optional: Raw cheese

Pepper and Salt

Instructions

1. Heat the oven to 400ºF.

2. Use medium heat on the stovetop; place an iron or oven-safe skillet. Crumble and brown the sausage. Remove the sausage, cook the potatoes until crunchy, and reserve the grease.

3. Put the sausage back in the pan. Make some spaces in the 'wells' of the skillet, enough room for one egg. Crack the eggs into each of the wells.

4. Put the skillet into the preheated oven and bake enough for the eggs to set (about 5 minutes). Turn up the thermostat in the oven

to the broil setting to let it broil the tops of the yolks with the crispy sweet potatoes.

5. Take the skillet out of the oven and cover it with some cilantro, avocado, and hot sauce.

Enjoy the tasty different flavors.

Cream Cheese Pancakes

Ingredients for the Pancakes

2 oz. (room temperature) cream cheese

2 organic eggs

½ teaspoon cinnamon

1 teaspoon granulated sugar substitute

Instructions

1. Place each of the pancake ingredients into a blender. Blend until creamy smooth; letting it rest for two minutes for the bubbles to settle back down.

2. Grease a pan with Pam spray or butter.

3. Pour about ¼ of the pancake batter into the hot pan; cooking for two minutes. Flip and continue cooking about one more minute.

4. Serve with berries or a sugar-free syrup of your choice.

Yields: Four Pancakes

Serving Size: 1 Batch: Carbs 2.5 g net; Fat 29; Protein 17 g; Calories 344

Dairy-Free Latte

Ingredients

2 Tbsp. coconut oil

1 2/3 C. hot water

2 eggs

1 tsp. ground ginger/pumpkin pie spice

Splash of vanilla extract

Instructions

1. Use a stick blender to combine all of the ingredients.

2. If you want to replace the spices; you can use 1 tablespoon of instant coffee or cocoa.

Enjoy for a quick boost!

Yields: Two Servings

Keto Sausage Patties

Ingredients

1 teaspoon maple extract

2 tablespoons granular Swerve Sweetener

½ teaspoon pepper

1 pound ground pork

2 tablespoons sage (chopped fresh)

1/8 teaspoon cayenne

1 teaspoon salt

¼ teaspoon garlic powder

Instructions

1. Combine each of the ingredients in a large mixing container.

2. Shape the patties to about a one-inch thickness.

3. The recipe will make eight equal patties.

4. Add a small amount of olive oil or a dab of butter to a pan over medium heat. For each side, allow three to four minutes.

Serving Portion: 2 patties: Carbs 1.4 g; Fat: 11 g;

Protein: 21 g; Calories: 187

Keto Bacon

Use the Regular Oven

1. Preheat to 350 ºF.

2. Put the bacon on a baking tray. Bake 20 to 25
   minutes

3. Drain on a paper towel.

Use the Microwave

1. Put the bacon on paper towels in a single layer on
   a microwave-safe dish.

2. Use the high setting for four to six minutes.

Use the Skillet

1. Prepare the pan on the medium-low to medium.

2. Put the bacon into the pan single-layered.

3. Cook until the desired doneness is acquired.

Serving Portion: 2 slices: Fat: 19 g; Carbs 0.0 g; Protein:

7 g; Calories: 200

Mushroom Omelet

Ingredients

3 eggs

7/8 ounces shredded cheese

2 to 3 mushrooms

Optional: 1/5 of an onion

Pepper and salt to taste

For frying: 7/8 ounces butter

Instructions

1. Whisk the eggs with the pepper and salt, add the spices.

2. On the stovetop, use a frying pan to melt the butter. Pour in the eggs.

3. When the omelet begins to cook to firmness; sprinkle the mushrooms, cheese, and onion on top.

4. Ease the edges up using a spatula, and fold in half. Remove from the pan when golden brown.

If you are having brunch; add a crispy salad.

Yields: One serving

Chapter 4: Additional Lunch and Dinner Recipes

Deviled Eggs

With this tasty combination; it is hard to say breakfast or lunch; maybe brunch!

Ingredients

6 large eggs

¼ teaspoon yellow mustard

1 tablespoon mayonnaise

1 teaspoon paprika

Garnish: Parsley/salt/pepper

Optional

- ½ teaspoon cayenne pepper

- Several drops hot sauce

- 1 teaspoon cumin

Instructions

1. Slice the eggs lengthwise.

2. Mix the egg yolks with the rest of the

   ingredients.

3. Put the goodies inside the egg bed.

4. Sprinkle with condiments as desired.

Serving Portion: Fat: 20 g; Carbs 1 g; Protein: 19 g;

Calories: 265

Ham and Apple Flatbread

Crust Ingredients

¾ cup almond flour

2 cups grated mozzarella cheese (part-skim)

2 tablespoons cream cheese

1/8 teaspoon dried thyme

½ teaspoon sea salt

Topping Ingredients

4 ounces sliced ham (low-carb)

½ small red onion

1 cup grated Mexican cheese

¼ medium apple

1/8 teaspoon dried thyme

Instructions

1. Remove the seeds and core from the apples. You
    can leave them unpeeled but will need to use a
    vegetable peeler to make the thin slices.

2. Heat the oven to 425ºF.

3. Cut two pieces of parchment paper to fit into a 12-inch pizza pan (approximately two inches larger than the pan).

4. Use the high-heat setting and place a double boiler (water in the bottom pan), and bring the water to boiling. Lower the heat setting and add the cream cheese, mozzarella cheese, salt, thyme, and almond flour to the top of the double boiler—stirring constantly.

5. When the cheese mixture resembles dough, place it on one of the pieces of parchment—and knead the dough until totally mixed.

6. Roll the dough into a ball—placing it at the center of the paper—place the second piece of paper over the top, and roll with a rolling pin (or a large glass).

7. Place the dough onto the pizza pan (leaving the paper connected).

8. Poke several holes in the dough and put into the preheated oven for approximately six to eight minutes.

9. When browned, remove it, and lower the setting of the oven to 350ºF.

10. Arrange the cheese, apple slices, onion slices, and ham pieces.

11. Top off with the remainder (3/4 cup) of cheese.

12. Season with the ground pepper, salt, and thyme.

13. Place the finished product into the oven, baking until you see a golden brown crust.

14. Slide it from the parchment paper and cool two or three minutes before cutting.

Yields: Eight Slices

Tip: If you do not own a double boiler; you can substitute with a mixing dish over a pot of boiling water as a substitute.

Serving Portion: 1: Fat: 20 g; Carbs 5 g; Protein: 16 g; Calories: 255

Chicken Breast with Herb Butter

Ingredients for the Fried Chicken

4 Chicken Breasts

Pepper and Salt

1-ounce of olive oil/butter

Herb Butter Ingredients

1 clove garlic

1/3 Pound butter (room temperature)

1 tsp. lemon juice

½ tsp. each:

- garlic powder

- salt

4 Tbsp. fresh chopped parsley

Leafy Greens

½ Pound leafy greens (baby spinach for example)

Instructions

1. Take the butter out of the refrigerator for at least thirty to sixty minutes before you begin to prepare your meal.

2. Add all of the ingredients, including the butter, and blend thoroughly in a small container; set to the side.

3. Use the pepper and salt to flavor the chicken. Cook the chicken filets in a skillet using the butter over medium heat. To avoid dried out filets, lower the temperature the last few minutes.

4. Serve over a bed of greens with some melted herb butter over the top.

Yields: Four Servings

Low-Carbonara

Ingredients

2/3 Pounds diced Pancetta/bacon

1 ¼ cups heavy whipping cream

1 tablespoon butter

3 1/3 tablespoons mayonnaise

Fresh chopped parsley

Pepper and salt

2 Pounds zucchini

3 ½ ounces grated Parmesan cheese

4 egg yolks

Instructions

1. Empty the heavy cream into a saucepan, bringing it to a boil. Lower the burner and continue boiling until the juices are reduced by about a third.

2. Fry the bacon/pancetta; reserve the fat.

3. Combine the heavy cream, mayonnaise, pepper, and salt into the saucepan mixture.

4. Make 'zoodles' out of the zucchini using a potato peeler or spiralizer.

5. Add the zoodles to the warm sauce and serve with egg yolks, bacon, parsley, and freshly grated cheese.

6. Drizzle a bit of the bacon grease on top.

Yummy!

Yields: Four Servings

Pesto Chicken Casserole with Olives and Cheese

Ingredients

1 ½ Pounds chicken breasts/thighs

3 ½ ounces green or red pesto

8 tablespoons pitted olives

1 2/3 cups heavy whipping cream

½ Pound diced feta cheese

Pepper and Salt

1 finely chopped garlic clove

For Frying: Butter

For Serving

- Olive oil

- 1/3 Pound leafy greens

- Sea salt

Instructions

1. Heat the oven to 400ºF.

2. Cut the chicken into pieces and flavor with the pepper and salt.

3. Place in a skillet with the butter, cooking until well done.

4. Combine the heavy cream and pesto.

5. Put the chicken pieces in the baking dish with the garlic, feta cheese, and olives, along with the pesto mix.

6. Bake for 20 to 30 minutes until the perfect color.

Enjoy with some green beans, sautéed asparagus, or another veggie of your choice.

Yields: Four Servings

Red Pesto Pork Chops

Ingredients

4 Pork chops

4 tablespoons red pesto

2 tablespoons olive oil/butter

6 tablespoons mayonnaise

Instructions

1. Thoroughly rub the chops with the pesto.

2. Fry on medium heat in a skillet with oil/butter for eight minutes. Reduce the heat and simmer four more minutes.

3. Serve with the pesto mayonnaise: 6 tablespoons of mayonnaise (+) 1 to 2 tablespoons pesto.

Serve with a large salad. You can also add a serving of cauliflower and broccoli with cheese.

Chapter 5:

Snacks and Desserts for the Diet Plan

Keto Ginger Snap Cookies

Ingredients

¼ cup unsalted butter

1 large egg

2 C. almond flour

½ tsp. ground cinnamon

1 tsp. vanilla extract

1 C. sugar substitute/Erythritol (Swerve)

2 tsp. ground ginger

¼ tsp. each:

- Salt

- Ground cloves

- Nutmeg

Instructions

1. Set the oven to 350ºF.

2. Combine the dry ingredients in a small dish.

3. Combine the remainder components to the dry mixture, and mix using a hand blender/mixer. (The dough will be crumbly and stiff.)

4. Measure out the dough for each cookie and flatten with a fork or your fingers.

5. Bake for approximately nine to eleven minutes or till they are browned.

Yields: 24 Cookies

Pumpkin Pudding

Ingredients

¼ cup pumpkin puree

1/3 cup granulated (Erythritol/Stevia)

½ tsp. pumpkin pie spices

1 tsp. xanthan gum

3 medium egg yolks

1 ½ cups whipping cream

1 tsp. vanilla extract

For the Cream Mixture

3 Tbsp. granulated stevia

1 cup whipping cream

½ tsp. vanilla extract

Instructions

1. Blend the pumpkin spice, xanthan gum, sweetener, and salt. Whip/whisk until the texture is smooth. Add the yolks, puree, and vanilla extract to the mixture; blend thoroughly.

2. Slowly pour in the whipping cream, after all of the cream is added. Using medium heat let the mixture come to a boil.

3. Continue the process for about 4 to 7 minutes, until thickened.

4. Place in the refrigerator in a container. Stir every ten minutes.

5. Meanwhile, in a medium dish, use a mixer to whip the one cup of whipping cream resulting in stiff peaks. Add the vanilla and sweetener; stir gently.

6. After the base pudding mixture has cooled; fold the whipped cream into the mix.

Scoop the pudding into small serving dishes and chill for a minimum of one to two hours.

Note: The Xanthan gum is available on Amazon.

Yields: Six Servings

No-Bake Cashew Coconut Bars

Ingredients

¼ cup maple syrup/sugar-free

1 cup almond flour

¼ cup melted butter

1 teaspoon cinnamon

½ cup cashews

A pinch of salt

1/4 cup shredded coconut

Instructions

1. Combine the flour and melted butter in a large mixing dish.

2. Add the maple syrup, cinnamon, salt, and coconut —blend well.

3. Use roasted or raw cashews. Chop them and add to the cashew-coconut bar dough. Blend well again.

4. Cover a cookie pan with parchment paper and spread the dough onto the paper in an even layer.

5. Place in the fridge for a minimum of two hours. Slice them and enjoy!

Yields: Eight Servings

Brownie Cheesecake

The Brownie Base Ingredients:

2 ounces chopped unsweetened chocolate

2 large eggs

½ cup butter

1/2 cup almond flour

1 pinch of salt

¼ cup cocoa powder

¾ cup granulated Erythritol/Swerve Sweetener

¼ cup pecans/walnuts (chopped)

¼ teaspoon vanilla

Cheesecake Filling Ingredients

2 large eggs

1 pound softened cream cheese

½ cup granulated sugar/Swerve sweetener

½ teaspoon vanilla extract

¼ cup heavy cream

Instructions

1. Butter a nine-inch springform pan; wrapping the bottom with foil.

2. Set the oven at 325ºF.

3. Melt the chocolate and butter in a microwave-safe dish for 30 seconds.

4. Whisk the cocoa powder, almond flour, and salt in a small dish.

5. In a separate dish; whip the vanilla, eggs, and Swerve until smooth.

6. Blend the flour mixture and chocolate/butter mixture. Blend in the nuts.

7. Spread out in the prepared dish and bake for approximately 15 to 20 minutes.

8. Let it cool for about 20 to 25 minutes.

For the Filling

1. Reduce the oven setting to 300ºF.

2. Blend the Swerve, the vanilla, cream, eggs, and cream cheese in a mixing container until everything is thoroughly mixed. Empty the filling ingredients into the crust and place it on a large cookie sheet.

3. Bake for about 35 to 45 minutes. The center should barely jiggle.

4. Loosen the edges with a knife.

5. Place them in the fridge for a minimum of three hours.

Yields: Ten Servings

Chocolate Soufflé

Ingredients

1/3 cup sugar substitute (Lakanto Mont Fruit/Amazon)

1 tablespoon butter

6 large egg whites

3 large egg yolks

5 ounces unsweetened chocolate

Note: The eggs work best at room temperature.

Instructions

1. Preset the oven to 375ºF.

2. Use the butter to grease a soufflé dish.

3. Use a double boiler or a metal dish above a pan of boiling water to melt the chocolate. (Stir the mix constantly.)

4. Remove the dish and whip in the yolks until the mix hardens. Set it to the side.

5. Use a pinch of salt, whip/whisk the egg whites with an electric mixer on the highest setting.

6. Gradually, blend in the sugar/Lakanto. Continue until you see stiff peaks.

7. Stir in one cup of the egg whites into the chocolate combination folding gently using a silicone spatula. Pour the mixture into the soufflé dish.

8. Bake approximately twenty minutes. The center should still jiggle with the soufflé crusted and puffed on the top.

Serve this delicious treat right away.

Topping/Optional: Coconut whipped cream

Yields: Four Treats

Note: To make the soufflé rise evenly; use your thumb to remove the batter from the top of the dish.

Macaroon Keto Bombs

Your curiosity is wondering, "What is a bomb?" The reasoning is that this is good for you and is too delicious to pass by when you are craving a treat!

Ingredients

½ cup shredded coconut

¼ cup almond flour

2 tablespoons sugar substitute (Swerve)

3 egg whites

1 tablespoon each:

- Coconut oil

- Vanilla extract

Instructions

1. Set the oven at 400ºF.

2. In a small container, combine the almond flour, coconut, and Swerve.

3. Use a small saucepan to melt the coconut oil. Add the vanilla extract.

4. *Note*: To mount the egg whites, place a medium dish in the freezer.

5. Add the oil to the flour mixture and blend well.

6. Break the egg whites in the cold dish and whip until stiff peaks are formed. Blend the egg whites into the flour mixture.

7. Spoon the mixture into a muffin cup or place them on a baking sheet.

8. Bake the macaroons for eight minutes or until you see browned edges.

9. Cool the bombs before you attempt to remove them from the pan.

Yields: Ten Servings

Conclusion

Thank for viewing your personal copy of the *Ketogenic Diet: Better Energy, Performance, and Natural Fuel to Good Health for the Smart.* Let's hope it was informative and able to provide you with all of the tools you need to achieve your goals as a better energy management specialist.

The next step is to test some of the recipes for yourself and discover what you have been missing since you have tried so many times unsuccessfully using other dieting methods. The recipes provided have been tested by qualified chefs who know the deal when it comes to energy performance.

Just remember, making advances towards a better lifestyle begins at the breakfast, lunch, and dinner table. You can supplement as you see fit once you have the knack of how the balance works.

Index for Recipes

Chapter 2: The 14-Day Plan

Day One

- Breakfast: Keto Scrambled Eggs
- Lunch: Tuna Cheese Melt (Low-Carbs)
- "Oopsie" Bread
- Dinner: Chicken Smothered in Creamy Onion Sauce

Day Two

- Breakfast: Mock Mc Griddle Casserole
- Brussels Sprouts with Hamburger Gratin
- Dinner: Squash and Sausage Casserole

Day Three

- Breakfast: Can't Beat it Porridge
- Lunch: Salad From a Jar
- Dinner: Ham and Cheese Stromboli

Day Four

- Breakfast: Frittata with Cheese and Tomatoes

- Lunch: Chicken—Broccoli—Zucchini Boats

- Dinner: Steak-Lovers Slow-Cooked Chili

Day 5

- Breakfast: Brownie Muffins

- Lunch: Bacon-Avocado-Goat Cheese Salad

- Dinner: Tenderloin Stuffed Keto Style

Day 6

- Breakfast: Sausage—Feta—Spinach Omelet

- Lunch: Pancakes with Cream-Cheese Topping

- Dinner: Skillet Style Sausage and Cabbage Melt

Day 7

- Breakfast: Tapas

- Lunch: Tofu—Bok-Choy Salad

- Dinner: Hamburger Stroganoff

Day 8

- Breakfast: Cheddar—Jalapeno Waffles

- Lunch: Salmon Tandoori with Cucumber Sauce

- Dinner: Ground Beef Stir Fry

Day 9

- Breakfast: Cheddar and Sage Waffles

- Lunch: Crispy Shrimp Salad on an Egg Wrap

- Dinner: Bacon Wrapped Meatloaf

Day 10

- Breakfast: Omelet Wrap with Avocado & Salmon

- Lunch: Tuna Avocado Melt

- Dinner: Hamburger Patties with Fried Cabbage

Day 11

- Breakfast: The Breadless Breakfast Sandwich

- Lunch: Thai Fish With Coconut & Curry

- Dinner: Keto Tacos or Nachos

Day 12

- Breakfast: Scrambled Eggs With Halloumi Cheese

- Lunch: Salmon with Spinach and Chili Tones

- Dinner: Chicken Stuffed Avocado—Cajun Style

Day 13

- Breakfast: Western Omelet

- Lunch: Tortilla Ground Beef Salsa

- Low-Carb Tortillas

- Dinner: Fish Casserole with Mushrooms

Day 14

- Breakfast: Blueberry Smoothie

- Lunch: Cheeseburger

- Dinner: Turkey with Cream Cheese Sauce

Chapter 3: Additional Breakfast Recipes

- Chia Pudding

- Cow-time Breakfast Skillet

- Cream Cheese Pancakes

- Dairy Free Latte

- Keto Sausage Patties

- Keto Bacon

- Mushroom Omelet

Chapter 4: Additional Lunch and Dinner Recipes

- Deviled Eggs

- Ham and Apple Flatbread

- Chicken Breast with Herb Butter

- Low-Carbonara

- Pesto Chicken Casserole with Olives and Cheese

- Red Pesto Pork Chops

Chapter 5: Snacks and Desserts for the Diet Plan

- Keto Ginger Snap Cookies

- Pumpkin Pudding

- No-Bake Cashew Coconut Bars

- Brownie Cheesecake

- Chocolate Soufflé

Macaroon Keto Bombs

THE 10 DAY KETOGENIC CLEANSE

INCREASE YOUR METABOLISM AND

DETOX WITH THESE DELICIOUS AND FUN IN A FAST 10 DAY MEAL PLAN

DIANA WATSON

DEDICATION

CONTENTS

ACKNOWLEDGMENTS

INTRODUCTION

Hello, dear reader! We are immensely thankful you are interested in improving your health and fitness by utilizing the methods involved in a ketogenic diet. It is our hope that your determination combined with our thorough meal plan and wonderful recipes will give you a jump start toward your fitness goals. You may have opened this book with a question in mind, "What in the world is a ketogenic cleanse, anyway?" Well, we are glad you asked! A ketogenic cleanse is inspired by the methods of a ketogenic diet. A ketogenic diet aims to change your body's metabolic focus from carbohydrate- based to fat-based fuels in order to produce cellular energy. Its aim is to develop healthy eating habits by replacing useless foods with the nutrients and fuel your body actually needs. This book contains further information about ketogenic dieting and a ten day meal plan accompanied by easy recipes. Having access to a meal plan is one of the most effective ways you can stay motivated along your ketogenic diet journey. So put on your apron, grab your greens, and head to the kitchen for some fat burning, healthy living!

CHAPTER 1: KETO BASICS

In the introduction we briefly discussed the meaning and theory behind ketogenic dieting. Here we will delve further into the science behind the method and how it can boost your metabolism and detox your body in 10 days.

BENEFITS OF INCREASED METABOLISM

One of the best ways to learn the meaning of a scientific term is to break it down to its roots. When we break down ketogenic we see it is comprised of two words: keto and genic. Ketones are fat-based molecules that the body breaks down when it is using fat as its energy source. When used as a suffix, "genic" means "causing, forming, or producing". So, we put these terms together and we have "ketogenic", or simply put, "causing fat burn". Ergo, the theory behind ketogenic dieting is: when a person reduces the amount of sugar and carbohydrates they consume, the body will begin to breakdown fat it already has in stores all over the body. When your body is cashing in on these stores, it is in a ketogenic state, or "ketosis". When your body consumes food, it naturally seeks carbohydrates for the purpose of breaking them down and using them as fuel. Adversely, a ketogenic cleanse trains your body to use fats for energy instead. This is achieved by lowering the amount of ingested carbohydrates and increasing the amount of ingested fats, which in turn boosts your metabolism.

Only recently has a low carb- high fat diet plan emerged into the public eye. It is a sharp contrast to the traditional dieting style that emphasizes calorie counting. For many years it was over looked that crash diets neglect the most important aspect of dieting: food is fuel. A diet is not meant be treated as a once a year go to method in order to shed holiday weight in January. Rather, a diet is a lifestyle; it is a consistent pattern of how an individual fuels their body. A ten day ketogenic cleanse is the perfect way to begin forming healthy eating habits that overtime become second nature. If you are tired of losing weight just to gain it all back, never fear. We firmly believe that you can accomplish anything you put your mind to, including living a healthy life! You, like hundreds of others, can successfully accomplish a ketogenic cleanse and change the way you see health, fitness, and life along the way. So let's hit the books and get that metabolism working!

BENEFITS OF CLEANSING

In addition to increased metabolism and fat loss, ketogenic cleansing allows your body naturally rid itself of harmful toxins and wasteful substances. In today's modern world, food is overrun and polluted by genetically modified hormones, artificial flavors and coloring, and copious amounts of unnecessary sugars. Ketogenic cleansing eliminates breads, grains, and many other foods that are most affected by today's modern industrialization. Due to the high amount of naturally occurring foods used in a ketogenic cleanse, the body is able to obtain many vitamins and minerals that are not prevalent in a high carb diet. When the body is consuming sufficient amounts of necessary vitamins and minerals, it is able to heal itself and maintain a healthy immune system. Cleansing your body is one of the best ways to achieve, and maintain, pristine health.

CHAPTER 2: MEAL PLAN MADNESS

One of the best ways to stay motivated, when dieting, is to find a meal plan that is easy to follow and easy on the budget. Ketogenic meals are designed to be filling while keeping within the perimeters of low-carb, high-fat guidelines. Ideally you want to aim for 70% fats, 25% protein, and 5% carbohydrates in your diet. As long as the materials you use to build your meals are low in carbs and high in fats, feel free to experiment and find what is right for you. Each and every one of us is different and that's okay. After all, this meal plan is for YOU!

Below is a ten day meal plan, designed with a busy schedule in mind, which will not break the bank! All of these meals can be prepared in 30 minutes or less, and many of them are much quicker than that! There is also a list of ingredients for each meal located in the recipe chapter so you can go to the

grocery store knowing exactly what you need!

	Breakfast	**Lunch**	**Dinner**
Day 1	**California Chicken Omelet** • Fat: 32 grams • 10 minutes to prepare • Protein: 25 grams • 10 minutes of cooking • Net carbs: 4 grams	**Cobb Salad** • Fat: 48 grams • 10 minutes to prepare • Protein: 43 grams • 0 minutes of cooking • Net carbs: 3 grams	**Chicken Peanut Pad Thai** • Fat: 12 grams • 15 minutes to prepare • Protein: 30 grams • 15 minutes of cooking • Net carbs: 2 grams
Day 2	**Easy Blender Pancakes** • Fat: 29 grams • 5 minutes to prepare • Protein: 41 grams • 10	**Sardine Stuffed Avocados** • Fat: 29 grams • 10 minutes to prepare • Protein: 27 grams • 0 minutes of cooking • Net Carbs: 5 grams	**Chipotle Fish Tacos** • Fat: 20 grams • 5 minutes to prepare • Protein: 24 grams • 15 minutes of cooking • Net carbs: 5 grams

	minutes of cooking • Net carbs: 4 grams		
Day 3	**Steak and Eggs** • Fat: 36 grams • 10 minutes to prepare • Protein: 47 grams • 5 minutes of cooking • Net carbs: 3 grams	**Low-Carb Smoothie Bowl** • Fat 35 grams • 5 minutes to prepare • Protein: 20 grams • 0 minutes of cooking • Net carbs: 5 grams	**Avocado Lime Salmon** • Fat: 27 grams • 20 minutes to prepare • Protein: 37 grams • 10 minutes of cooking • Net carbs: 5 grams
KEEP IT UP!!!	During the course of your plan, especially around days 3 and 4, you may begin to feel like you don't have it in you. You may have thoughts telling you that you cannot last for ten days on this type pf cleanse. Do not allow feelings of discouragement bother you because, guess what? We all feel that way sometimes! A ketogenic diet causes your body to process energy like it never has before. Keep pressing on! Your body will thank you and so will you!		
Day 4	**Low-Carb Smoothie Bowl**	**Pesto Chicken Salad**	**Siracha Lime Flank**

	<ul><li>Fat: 35 grams</li><li>5 minutes to prepare</li><li>Protein: 35 grams</li><li>0 minutes of cooking</li><li>Net carbs: 4 grams</li></ul>	<ul><li>Fat: 27 grams</li><li>5 minutes to prepare</li><li>Protein: 27 grams</li><li>10 minutes of cooking</li><li>Net carbs: 3 grams</li></ul>	**Steak**<ul><li>Fat: 32 grams</li><li>5 minutes to prepare</li><li>Protein: 48 grams</li><li>10 minutes of cooking</li><li>Net Carbs: 5 grams</li></ul>
Day 5	**Feta and Pesto Omelet**<ul><li>Fat: 46 grams</li><li>5 minutes of preparation</li><li>Protein: 30 grams</li><li>5 minutes of cooking</li><li>Net carbs: 2.5 grams</li></ul>	**Roasted Brussel Sprouts**<ul><li>Fat: 21 grams</li><li>5 minutes to prepare</li><li>Protein: 21 grams</li><li>30 minutes of cooking</li><li>Net carbs: 4 grams</li></ul>	**Low carb Sesame Chicken**<ul><li>Fat: 36 grams</li><li>15 minutes to prepare</li><li>Protein: 41 grams</li><li>15 minutes of cooking</li><li>Net carbs: 4 grams</li></ul>

Day 6	**Raspberry Cream Crepes** • Fat: 40 grams • 5 minutes of preparation • Net carbs: 8 grams • 15 minutes of cooking • Protein 15 grams	**Shakshuka** • Fat: 34 grams • Protein 35 grams • Net carbs: 4 grams • 10 minutes of preparation • 10 minutes of cooking	**Sausage in a Pan** • Fat: 38 grams • 10 minutes of preparation • Protein: 30 grams • 25 minutes of cooking • Net Carbs: 4 grams
Day 7	**Green Monster Smoothie** • Fat: 25 grams • 5 minutes of preparation • Protein: 30 grams • 0 minutes of cooking • Net Carbs: 3 grams	**Tuna Tartare** • Fat: 24 grams • 15 minutes of preparation • Protein: 56 grams • 0 minutes of cooking • Net Carbs: 4 grams	**Pesto Chicken Salad** • Fat: 27 grams • 5 minutes of preparation • Protein: 27 grams • 10 minutes of cooking • Net carbs: 3 grams

ALMOST THERE !!	By now, you can be certain you are seeing physical results such as reduced body fat and more energy! You are doing a fantastic job and you only have three days left! Keep up the good work, you owe it to yourself.		
Day 8	**Shakshuka** • Fat: 34 grams • 10 minutes of preparation • Protein 35 grams • 10 minutes of cooking • Net carbs: 4 grams	**Grilled Halloumi Salad** • Fat: 47 grams • 15 minutes of preparation • Protein: 21 grams • 0 minutes of cooking • Net carbs: 2 grams	**Keto Quarter Pounder** • Fat: 34 grams • 10 minutes of preparation • Protein: 25 grams • 8 minutes of cooking • Net carbs: 4 •
Day 9	**Easy Blender Pancakes** • Fat: 29 grams • 5 minutes of preparation • Protein: 41	**Broccoli Bacon Salad** • Fat: 31 grams • 15 minutes of preparation • Protein: 10 grams • 6 minutes of cooking • Net carbs: 5 grams	**Sardine Stuffed Avocados** • Fat: 29 grams • 10 minutes to prepare • Protein: 27

	- grams - 10 minutes of cooking - Net carbs: 4 grams		- grams - 0 minutes to cook - Net Carbs: 5 grams
Day 10	**California Chicken Omelet** - Fat 32 grams - 10 minutes to prepare - Protein 25 grams - 10 minutes of cooking - Net carb: 3 grams	**Shrimp Scampi** - Fat: 21 grams - 5 minutes to prepare - Protein: 21 grams - 30 minutes of cooking - Net carbs: 4 grams	**Tuna Tartare** - Fat: 36 grams - 15 minutes to prepare - Protein: 41 grams - 15 minutes of cooking - Net carbs: 4 grams
YOU DID IT!!	Congratulations! You have successfully completed a 10 day ketogenic cleanse. By now your body has adjusted to its new source of energy, expelled dozens of harmful toxins, and replenished itself with many vitamins and minerals it may have been lacking. Way to go on a job well done!		

CHAPTER 3: BREAKFAST IS FOR CHAMPIONS

Breakfast is by far the most important meal of the day for one reason: it set the tone for the rest of your day. In order to hit the ground running, it is vital that one starts each day with foods that fuel an energetic and productive day. This chapter contains ten ketogenic breakfast ides that will have you burning fat and conquering your day like you never imagined.

1. CALIFORNIA CHICKEN OMELET

- This recipe requires 10 minutes of preparation, 10 minutes of cooking time and serves 1

- Net carbs: 4 grams

- Protein: 25 grams

- Fat : 32 grams

What you will need:

- Mayo (1 tablespoon)

- Mustard (1 teaspoon)

- Campari tomato

- Eggs (2 large beaten)

- Avocado (one fourth, sliced)

- Bacon (2 slices cooked and chopped)

- Deli chicken (1 ounce)

What to do:

1. Place a skillet on the stove over a burner set to a medium heat and let it warm before adding in the eggs and seasoning as needed.

2. Once eggs are cooked about halfway through, add bacon, chicken, avocado, tomato, mayo, and mustard on one side of the eggs.

3. Fold the omelet onto its self, cover and cook for 5 additional minutes.

4. Once eggs are fully cooked and all ingredients
   are warm, through the center, your omelet is
   ready.

5. Bon apatite!

2. STEAK AND EGGS WITH AVOCADO

- This recipe requires 10 minutes of preparation, 5 minutes of cooking time and serves 1

- Net Carbs: 3 grams

- Protein: 44 grams

- Fat: 36 grams

What you will need:

- Salt and pepper

- Avocado (one fourth, sliced)

- Sirloin steak (4 ounce)

- Eggs (3 large)

- Butter (1 tablespoon)

What to do:

1. Melt the tablespoon of butter in a pan and fry
   all 3 eggs to desired doneness. Season the
   eggs with salt and pepper.

2. In a different pan, cook the sirloin steak to
   your preferred taste and slice it into thin
   strips. Season the steak with salt and pepper.

3. Sever your prepared steak and eggs with
   slices of avocado.

4. Enjoy!

3. PANCAKES IN A BLENDER

- This recipe requires 5 minutes of preparation,
  10 minutes of cooking time and serves 1

- Net Carbs: 4 grams

- Protein: 41 grams

- Fat: 29 grams

What you will need:

- Whey protein powder (1 scoop)

- Eggs (2 large)

- Cream cheese (2 ounces)

- Just a pinch of cinnamon and a pinch of salt

What to do:

1. Combine cream cheese, eggs, protein powder, cinnamon, and salt into a blender. Blend for 10 seconds and let stand.

2. While letting batter stand, warm a skillet over medium heat.

3. Pour about ¼ of the batter onto warmed skillet and let cook. When bubbles begin to emerge on the surface, flip the pancake.

4. Once flipped, cook for 15 seconds. Repeat until remainder of the batter is used up.

5. Top with butter and/ or sugar- free maple syrup and you are all set!

6. Chow time!

4. LOW CARB SMOOTHE BOWL

- Net Carbs: 4 grams

- Protein: 35 grams

- Fat: 35 grams

- Takes 5 minutes to prepare and serves 1.

What you will need:

- Spinach (1 cup)

- Almond milk (half a cup)

- Coconut oil (1 tablespoon)

- Low carb protein powder (1 scoop)

- Ice cubes (2 cubes)

- Whipping cream (2 T)

- Optional toppings can include: raspberries, walnuts, shredded coconut, or chia seeds

What to do:

1. Place spinach in blender. Add almond milk, cream, coconut oil, and ice. Blend until thoroughly and evenly combined.

2. Pour into bowl.

3. Top with toppings or stir lightly into smoothie.

4. Treat yourself!

5. FETA AND PESTO OMELET

- This recipe requires 5 minutes of preparation, 5 minutes of cooking time and serves 1

- Net Carbs: 2.5 grams

- Protein: 30 grams

- Fat: 46 grams

What you will need:

- Butter (1 tablespoon)

- Eggs (3 large)

- Heavy cream (1 tablespoon)

- Feta cheese (1 ounce)

- Basil pesto (1 teaspoon)

- Tomatoes (optional)

What to do:

1. Heat pan and melt butter.

2. Beat eggs together with heavy whipping cream (will give eggs a fluffy consistency once cooked).

3. Pour eggs in pan and cook until almost done, add feta and pesto to on half of eggs.

4. Fold omelet and cook for an additional 4-5 minutes.

5. Top with feta and tomatoes, and eat up!

6. CREPES WITH CREAM AND RASPBERRIES

- This recipe requires 5 minutes of preparation, 15 minutes of cooking time and serves 2

- Net Carbs: 8 grams

- Protein: 15 grams

- Fat: 40 grams

What you will need:

- Raspberries (3 ounces, fresh or frozen)

- Whole Milk Ricotta (half a cup and 2 tablespoons)

- Erythritol (2 tablespoons)

- Eggs (2 large)

- Cream Cheese (2 ounces)

- Pinch of salt

- Dash of Cinnamon

- Whipped cream and sugar- free maple syrup to go on top

What to do:

1. In a blender, blend cream cheese, eggs, erythritol, salt, and cinnamon for about 20 seconds, or until there are no lumps of cream cheese.

2. Place a pan on a burner turned to a medium heat before coating in cooking spray. Add 20 percent of your batter to the pan in a thin layer. Cook crepe until the underside becomes slightly darkened. Carefully flip the crepe and let the reverse side cook for about 15 seconds.

3. Repeat step 3 until all batter is used.

4. Without stacking the crepes, allow them to cool for a few minutes.

5. After the crepes have cool, place about 2 tablespoons of ricotta cheese in the center of each crepe.

6. Throw in a couple of raspberries and fold the side to the middle.

7. Top those off with some whipped cream and sugar- free maple syrup and...

8. Viola! You're a true chef! Indulge in your creation!

7. GREEN MONSTER SMOOTHIE

- This recipe requires 10 minutes of preparation, 0 minutes of cooking time and serves 1

- Net Carbs: 4 grams

- Protein: 30 grams

- Fat: 25 grams

What you will need:

- Almond milk (one and a half cups)

- Spinach (one eighth of a cup)

- Cucumber (fourth of a cup)

- Celery (fourth of a cup)

- Avocado (fourth of a cup)

- Coconut oil (1 tablespoon)

- Stevia (liquid, 10 drops)

- Whey Protein Powder (1 scoop)

What to do:

1. In a blender, blend almond milk and spinach
    for a few pulses.

2. Add remaining ingredients and blend until
    thoroughly combined.

3. Add optional matcha powder, if desired, and
    enjoy!

CHAPTER 4: LUNCH CRUNCH

Eating a healthy lunch when you are limited on time due to, work, school, or taking care of your kids can be a tumultuous task. Thankfully, we have compiled a list of eight quick and easy recipes to accompany the ten day meal plan laid out in chapter 2! Many find it advantageous, especially if you work throughout the week, to prepare you meals ahead of time. Thankfully, these lunch recipes are also easy to pack and take on the go!

1. OFF THE COBB SALAD

- Net carbs: 3 grams

- Protein: 43 grams

- Fat: 48 grams

- Takes 10 minutes to prepare and serves 1.

What you will need:

- Spinach (1 cup)

- Egg (1, hard-boiled)

- Bacon (2 strips)

- Chicken breast (2 ounces)

- Campari tomato (one half of tomato)

- Avocado (one fourth, sliced)

- White vinegar (half of a teaspoon)

- Olive oil (1 tablespoon)

What to do:

1. Cook chicken and bacon completely and cut or slice into small pieces.

2. Chop remaining ingredients into bite size pieces.

3. Place all ingredients, including chicken and bacon, in a bowl, toss ingredients in oil and vinegar.

4. Enjoy!

2. AVOCADO AND SARDINES

- Net Carbs: 5 grams

- Protein: 27 grams

- Fat: 52 grams

- Takes 10 minutes to prepare and serves 1.

What you will need:

- Fresh lemon juice (1 tablespoon)

- Spring onion or chives (1 or small bunch)

- Mayonnaise (1 tablespoon)

- Sardines (1 tin, drained)

- Avocado (1 whole, seed removed)

- Turmeric powder (fourth of a teaspoon) or freshly ground turmeric root (1 teaspoon)

- Salt (fourth of a teaspoon)

What to do:

1. Begin by cutting the avocado in half and removing its seed.

2. Scoop out about half the avocado and set aside (shown below).

3. In small bowl, mash drained sardines with fork.

4. Add onion (or chives), turmeric powder, and mayonnaise. Mix well.

5. Add removed avocado to sardine mixture.

6. Add lemon juice and salt.

7. Scoop the mixture into avocado halves.

8. Dig in!

3. CHICKEN SALAD A LA PESTO

- This recipe requires 5minutes of preparation, 10 minutes of cooking time and serves 4

- Net Carbs: 3 grams

- Protein: 27 grams

- Fat: 27 grams

What you will need:

- Garlic pesto (2 tablespoons)

- Mayonnaise (fourth of a cup)

- Grape tomatoes (10, halved)

- Avocado (1, cubed)

- Bacon (6 slices, cooked crisp and crumbled)

- Chicken (1 pound, cooked and cubed)

- Romaine lettuce (optional)

What to do:

1. Combine all ingredients in a large mixing bowl.

2. Toss gently to spread mayonnaise and pesto evenly throughout.

3. If desired, wrap in romaine lettuce for a low-carb BLT chicken wrap.

4. Bon apatite!

4. BACON AND ROASTED BRUSSEL SPROUTS

- This recipe requires 5 minutes of preparation, 30 minutes of cooking time and serves 4

- Net Carbs: 4 grams

- Protein: 15 grams

- Fat: 21 grams

What you will need:

- Bacon (8 strips)

- Olive oil (2 tablespoons)

- Brussel sprouts (1 pound, halved)

- Salt and pepper

What to do:

1. Preheat oven to 375 degrees Fahrenheit.

2. Gently mix Brussel sprouts with olive oil, salt, and pepper.

3. Spread Brussel sprouts evenly onto a greased baking sheet.

4. Bake in oven for 30 minutes. Shake the pan about halfway through to mix the Brussel sprout halves up a bit.

5. While Brussel sprouts are in the oven, fry bacon slices on stovetop.

6. When bacon is fully cooked, let cool and chop it into bite size pieces.

7. Combine bacon and Brussel sprouts in a bowl and you're finished!

8. Feast!!

5. GRILLED HALLOUMI SALAD

- Net Carbs: 7 grams

- Protein: 21 grams

- Fat: 47 grams

- Takes 15 minutes to prepare and serves 1.

What you will need:

- Chopped walnuts (half of an ounce)

- Baby arugula (1 handful)

- Grape tomatoes (5)

- Cucumber (1)

- Halloumi cheese (3 ounces)

- Olive oil (1 teaspoon)

- Balsamic vinegar (half of a teaspoon)

- A pinch of salt

What to do:

1. Slice halloumi cheese into slices 1/3 of an in
    thick.

2. Grill cheese for 3 to 5 minutes, until you see
    grill lines, on each side.

3. Wash and cut veggies into bite size pieces,
    place in salad bowl.

4. Add rinsed baby arugula and walnuts to
    veggies.

5. Toss in olive oil, balsamic vinegar, and salt.

6. Place grilled halloumi on top of veggies and
    your lunch is ready!

7. Eat those greens and get back to work!

6. BACON BROCCOLI SALAD

- This recipe requires 15 minutes of preparation, 6 minutes of cooking time and serves 5.

- Net Carbs: 5 grams

- Protein: 10 grams

- Fat: 31 grams

What you will need:

- Sesame oil (half of a teaspoon)

- Erythritol (1 and a half tablespoons) or stevia to taste

- White vinegar (1 tablespoon)

- Mayonnaise (half of a cup)

- Green onion (three fourths of an ounce)

- Bacon (fourth of a pound)

- Broccoli (1 pound, heads and stalks cut and trimmed)

What to do:

1. Cook bacon and crumble into bits.

2. Cut broccoli into bite sized pieces.

3. Slice scallions.

4. Mix mayonnaise, vinegar, erythritol (or stevia), and sesame oil, to make the dressing.

5. Place broccoli and bacon bits in a bowl and toss with dressing.

6. Viola!

7. TUNA AVOCADO TARTARE

- Net Carbs: 4 grams

- Protein: 56 grams

- Fat: 24 grams

- Takes 15 minutes to prepare and serves 2.

What you will need:

- Sesame seed oil (2 tablespoons)

- Sesame seeds (1 teaspoon)

- Cucumbers (2)

- Lime (half of a whole lime)

- Mayonnaise (1 tablespoon)

- Sriracha (1 tablespoon)

- Olive oil (2 tablespoons)

- Jalapeno (one half of whole jalapeno)

- Scallion (3 stalks)

- Avocado (1)

- Tuna steak (1 pound)

\-   Soy sauce (1 tablespoon)

What to do:

1. Dice tuna and avocado into ¼ inch cubes, place in bowl.

2. Finely chop scallion and jalapeno, add to bowl.

3. Pour olive oil, sesame oil, siracha, soy sauce, mayonnaise, and lime into bowl.

4. Using hands, toss all ingredients to combine evenly. Using a utensil may breakdown avocado, which you want to remain chunky, so it is best to use your hands.

5. Top with sesame seeds and serve with a side of sliced cucumber.

6. There's certainly something fishy about this recipe, but it tastes great! Enjoy!

8. WARM SPINACH AND SHRIMP

- This recipe requires 15 minutes of preparation, 6 minutes of cooking time and serves 5.

- Fat: 24 grams

- Protein: 36 grams

- Net Carbs: 3 grams

- Takes10 minutes to prepare, 5 minutes to cook, and serves 2.

What you will need:

- Spinach (2 handfuls)

- Parmesan (half a tablespoon)

- Heavy cream (1 tablespoon)

- Olive oil (1 tablespoon)

- Butter (2 tablespoons)

- Garlic (3 cloves)

- Onion (one fourth of whole onion)

- Large raw shrimp (about 20)

- Lemon (optional)

What to do:

1. Place peeled shrimp in cold water.

2. Chop onions and garlic into fine pieces.

3. Heat oil, in pan, over medium heat. Cook shrimp in oil until lightly pink (we do not want them fully cooked here). Remove shrimp from oil and set aside.

4. Place chopped onions and garlic into pan, cook until onions are translucent. Add a dash of salt.

5. Add butter, cream, and parmesan cheese. Stir until you have a smooth sauce.

6. Let sauce cook for about 2 minutes so it will thicken slightly.

7. Place shrimp back into pan and cook until done. This should take no longer than 2 or 3

minutes. Be careful not to overcook the

shrimp, it will become dry and tough!

8. Remove shrimp and sauce from pan and

replace with spinach. Cook spinach VERY

briefly

9. Place warmed spinach onto a plate.

10. Pour shrimp and sauce over bed of spinach,

squeeze some lemon on top, if you like, and

you're ready to chow down!

CHAPTER 5: THINNER BY DINNER

It's the end of the day and you are winding down from a hard day's work. Your body does not require a lot of energy while you sleep; therefore, dinner will typically consist of less fat and more protein.

1. CHICKEN PAD THAI

- Net Carbs: 7 grams

- Protein: 30 grams

- Fat: 12 grams

- Takes 15 minutes to prepare, 15 minutes to cook, and serves 4.

What you will need:

- Peanuts (1 ounce)

- Lime (1 whole)

- Soy sauce (2 tablespoons)

- Egg (1 large)

- Zucchini (2 large)

- Chicken thighs (16 ounces, boneless and skinless)
- Garlic (2 cloves, minced)
- White onion (1,chopped)
- Olive oil (1 tablespoon)
- Chili flakes (optional)

What to do:

1. Over medium heat, cook olive oil and onion until translucent. Add the garlic and cook about three minutes (until fragrant).
2. Cook chicken in pan for 5 to 7 minutes on each side (until fully cooked). Remove chicken from heat and shred it using a couple of forks.
3. Cut ends off zucchini and cut into thin noodles. Set zucchini noodles aside.
4. Next, scramble the egg in the pan.
5. Once the egg is fully cooked, and the zucchini noodles and cook for about 2 minutes.

6. Add the previously shredded chicken to the
   pan.

7. Give it some zing with soy sauce, lime juice,
   peanuts, and chili flakes.

8. Time to eat!

2. CHIPOTLE STYLE FISH TACOS

- Fat: 20 grams

- Protein: 24 grams

- Net Carbs: 7 grams

- Takes 5 minutes to prepare, 15 minutes to cook, and serves 4.

What you will need:

- Low carb tortillas (4)

- Haddock fillets (1 pound)

- Mayonnaise (2 tablespoons)

- Butter (2 tablespoons)

- Chipotle peppers in adobo sauce (4 ounces)

- Garlic (2 cloves, pressed)

- Jalapeño (1 fresh, chopped)

- Olive oil (2 tablespoons)

- Yellow onion (half of an onion, diced)

What to do:

1. Fry diced onion (until translucent) in olive oil
   in a high sided pan, over medium- high heat.

2. Reduce heat to medium, add jalapeno and
   garlic. Cook while stir for another two
   minutes.

3. Chop the chipotle peppers and add them,
   along with the adobo sauce, to the pan.

4. Add the butter, mayo, and fish fillets to the
   pan.

5. Cook the fish fully while breaking up the fillets
   and stirring the fish into other ingredients.

6. Warm tortillas for 2 minutes on each side.

7. Fill tortillas with fishy goodness and eat up!

3. SALMON WITH AVOCADO LIME SAUCE

- Net Carbs: 5 grams

- Protein: 37 grams

- Fat: 27 grams

- Takes 20 minutes to prepare, 10 minutes to cook, and serves 2.

What you will need:

- Salmon (two 6 ounce fillets)

- Avocado (1 large)

- Lime (one half of a whole lime)

- Red onion (2 tablespoons, diced)

- Cauliflower (100 grams)

What to do:

1. Chop cauliflower in a blender or food processor then cook it in a lightly oiled pan,

while covered, for 8 minutes. This will make
the cauliflower rice-like.

2. Next, blend the avocado with squeezed lime
juice in the blender or processor until smooth
and creamy.

3. Heat some oil in a skillet and cook salmon
(skin side down first) for 4 to 5 minute. Flip
the fillets and cook for an additional 4 to 5
minutes.

4. Place salmon fillet on a bed of your cauliflower
rice and top with some diced red onion.

4. SIRACHA LIME STEAK

- Net Carbs: 5 grams

- Protein: 48 grams

- Fat: 32 grams

- Takes 5 minutes to prepare, 10 minutes to cook, and serves 2.

What you will need:

- Vinegar (1 teaspoon)

- Olive oil (2 tablespoons)

- Lime (1 whole)

- Sriracha (2 tablespoons)

- Flank steak (16 ounce)

- Salt and pepper

What to do:

1. Season steak, liberally, with salt and pepper. Place on baking sheet, lined with foil, and broil in oven for 5 minutes on each side (add

another minute or two for a well done steak).

Remove from oven, cover, and set aside.

2. Place sriracha in small bowl and squeeze lime

into it. Whisk in salt, pepper, and vinegar.

3. Slowly pour in olive oil.

4. Slice steak into thin slices, lather on your

sauce, and enjoy!

5. Feel free to pair this recipe with a side of

greens such as asparagus or broccoli.

5. LOW CARB SESAME CHICKEN

- Net Carbs: 4 grams

- Protein: 45 grams

- Fat: 36 grams

- Takes 15minutes to prepare, 15 minutes to

cook, and serves 2.

What you will need:

- Broccoli (three fourths of a cup, cut bite size)

- Xanthan gum (fourth of a teaspoon)

- Sesame seeds (2 tablespoons)

- Garlic (1 clove)

- Ginger (1 cm cube)

- Vinegar (1 tablespoon)

- Brown sugar alternative (Sukrin Gold is a good one) (2 tablespoons)

- Soy sauce (2 tablespoons)

- Toasted sesame seed oil (2 tablespoons)

- Arrowroot powder or corn starch (1 tablespoon)

- Chicken thighs (1poundcut into bite sized pieces)

- Egg (1 large)

- Salt and pepper

- Chives (optional)

What to do:

1. First we will make the batter by combining the egg with a tablespoon of arrowroot powder (or cornstarch). Whisk well.

2. Place chicken pieces in batter. Be sure to coat all sides of chicken pieces with the batter.

3. Heat one tablespoon of sesame oil, in a large pan. Add chicken pieces to hot oil and fry. Be gentle when flipping the chicken, you want to keep the batter from falling off. It should take about 10 minutes for them to cook fully.

4. Next, make the sesame sauce. In a small bowl, combine soy sauce, brown sugar alternative, vinegar, ginger, garlic, sesame seeds, and the remaining tablespoon of toasted sesame seed oil. Whisk very well.

5. Once the chicken is fully cooked, add broccoli and the sesame sauce to pan and cook for an additional 5 minutes.

6. Spoon desired amount into a bowl, top it off with some chopped chives, and relish in some fine dining at home!

6. PAN 'O SAUSAGE

- Net Carbs: 4 grams

- Protein: 30 grams

- Fat: 38 grams

- Takes 10 minutes to prepare, 25 minutes to cook, and serves 2.

What you will need:

- Basil (half a teaspoon)

- Oregano (half a teaspoon)

- White onion (1 tablespoon)

- Shredded mozzarella (fourth of a cup)

- Parmesan cheese (fourth of a cup)

- Vodka sauce (half a cup)

- Mushrooms (4 ounces)

- Sausage (3 links)

- Salt (fourth of a teaspoon)

- Red pepper (fourth of a teaspoon, ground)

What to do:

1. Preheat oven to 350 degrees Fahrenheit.

2. Heat an iron skillet over medium flame. When skillet is hot, cook sausage links until almost thoroughly cooked.

3. While sausage is cooking, slice mushrooms and onion.

4. When sausage is almost fully cooked, remove links from heat and place mushrooms and onions in skillet to brown.

5. Cut sausage into pieces about ½ inch thick and place pieces in pan.

6. Season skillet contents with oregano, basil, salt, and red pepper.

7. Add vodka sauce and parmesan cheese. Stir everything together.

8. Place skillet in oven for 15 minutes. Sprinkle mozzarella on top a couple minutes before removing dish from oven.

9. Once 15 minutes is up, remove skillet from the

oven and let cool for a few minutes.

10. Dinner time!

7. QUARTER POUNDER KETO BURGER

- Net Carbs: 4 grams

- Protein: 25 grams

- Fat: 34 grams

- Takes 10 minutes to prepare, 8 minutes to cook, and serves 2.

What you will need:

- Basil (half a teaspoon)

- Cayenne (fourth a teaspoon)

- Crushed red pepper (half a teaspoon)

- Salt (half a teaspoon)

- Lettuce (2 large leaves)

- Butter (2 tablespoons)

- Egg (1 large)

- Sriracha (1 tablespoon)

- Onion (fourth of whole onion)

- Plum tomato (half of whole tomato)

- Mayo (1 tablespoon)

- Pickled jalapenos (1 tablespoon, sliced)

- Bacon (1 strip)

- Ground beef (half a pound)

- Bacon (1 strip)

What to do:

1. Knead mean for about three minute.

2. Chop bacon, jalapeno, tomato, and onion into fine pieces. (shown below)

3. Knead in mayo, sriracha, egg, and chopped ingredients, and spices into meat.

4. Separate meat into four even pieces and flatten them (not thinly, just press on the tops to create a flat surface). Place a tablespoon of butter on top of two of the meat pieces. Take the pieces that do not have butter of them and set them on top of the buttered ones (basically

creating a butter and meat sandwich). Seal the sides together, concealing the butter within.

5. Throw the patties on the grill (or in a pan) for about 5 minutes on each side. Caramelize some onions if you want too!

6. Prepare large leaves of lettuce by spreading some mayo onto them. Once patties are finished, place them on one half of the lettuce, add your desired burger toppings, and fold the other half over of the lettuce leaf over the patty.

7. Burger time!

CONCLUSION

THANK YOU FOR PURCHASING THIS BOOK. IT IS MY HOPE THAT YOU HAVE HAD AN INCREDIBLE EXPERIENCE IMPROVING YOUR HEALTH AND LEARNING NEW THINGS WHILE, MOST IMPORTANTLY, HAVING FUN ALONG THE WAY! EACH AND EVERY ONE OF US CAN BENEFIT FROM A KETOGENIC CLEANSE AND IT IS ABSOLUTELY FANTASTIC TO WITNESS PEOPLE BEING CONSCIOUS OF THEIR HEALTH AND TAKING CARE OF THEIR BODIES. WHETHER THE 10 DAY KETOGENIC CLEANSE HAS EMPOWERED YOU TO ADOPT AN ONGOING KETOGENIC DIET OR HAS SHOWN YOU IT IS NOT FOR YOU, I GREATLY APPRECIATE YOUR TIME IN READING THIS.

VIP Subscriber List

Hi Dear Reader, this is Diana! If you like my book and you want to receive the latest tips and tricks on cooking, weight-loss, cookbook recipes and more, do subscribe to my mailing list in the link here! I will then be able to send you the most up-to-date information about my upcoming books and promotions as well! Thank you for supporting my work and happy reading!

Subscriber Form

http://bit.do/dianawatson